# The Bite of Pleasure

## Adam and Eve's Secrets to Lasting Love

### Pastor Eddie Fray

Scripture references are taken from the Holy Bible: King James Version

ISBN: 978-0692978825


Published by Candy Publishing, LLC
www.candypublishing.net

*Printed in the United States of America*

Editor, Cynthia A. Fray

Cover Design, DK1 Promotions

# SPECIAL DEDICATION

To my first love, my mother
Mrs. Universe, Queen of all Queens,
Mrs. Evelyn Weaden

## DEDICATION

To the greatest of all of God's creation
"Women"

To everyone lacking fulfillment in their
relationship

To every married couple seeking to improve
their marriage

To the reader who discovers the secret keys to
satisfying their mate

To the reader who has the courage to
acknowledge
and embrace change.

# CONTENTS

# ACKNOWLEDGMENTS

To the creator of the universe for revelatory wisdom & knowledge.

To my wife, Cynthia A. Fray, the love of my life. Together still! Thank you for making our home a Garden of Eden and for allowing me to experience a portion of heaven on earth with you. Thank you for all the efforts you contributed to the completion of this project.

To my daughters, from infancy to adulthood you have been my motivation. To my granddaughter Karmin, set and maintain high standards.

To my mom, Evelyn Weaden. It was the early years that helped shape my views on love and marriage. Thank you for teaching me how to treat someone else's daughter.

To the only Dad I have ever known, Joseph Weaden. You were there when we so badly needed you. You made the road smoother and the load lighter.

To Diana Samuel, my only sister. You are everything a mother could hope for. Your perpetual sacrifices will not go un-rewarded. Thank you for being a good sister to your big brother.

To my brothers, Alex, Eric, Earl, and Ronald. We have gone through a lot, but we are still standing.

To my sister in law Anna Fray, thanks for giving me a different point of view on many subjects discussed.

Lastly, thanks to the Life Changing Ministries family, both present and former members.

# The Bite of Pleasure

Adam and Eve's Secrets to Lasting Love

**Pastor Eddie L. Fray**

Ladies,

Please, don't ever forget

YOU are God's gift to man

YOU are the prize!

# INTRODUCTION

When a woman pleases a man, and a man pleases a woman

## EXPLOSIVE POWER IS UNLEASHED!

This is not a book on how to have great sex, any adult can figure that out. Instead, *The Bite of Pleasure* is a book on how to experience an orgasmic relationship that leads to great sex. As you take this biblical, metaphorical journey coupled with the power of imagination, this inspiring book will take your marriage to a new level.

The title was derived from what transpired in the soul of Adam and Eve. Some amazing and astonishing occurrences to maintaining one's marriage took place in the Garden of Eden. The secrets and lost lessons of the Garden of Eden will be discussed as they relate to the marriage of today. God's standard for marriage originated in the Garden of Eden and once the standard is acknowledged and applied in your relationship, you'll experience a welcoming renewal, with your spouse, in every aspect of your love life. The first couple's brief and powerful encounter with the Creator, and with each other, holds the key to a loving and lasting relationship.

I don't consider myself a marriage or relationship expert, yet I've been blessed with a unique ability to dissect and discern the biblical standard as it relates to a sensual marriage. My knowledge *and* experience will be imparted in a way to ignite a stronger desire to master the art of pleasing your spouse.

Most men, including myself, take pride in being a good lover. Some will even say they are a great lover. Men who take pride in their ability to make love have learned to satisfy their woman first. If we accomplish on our feet what we hope to accomplish between the sheets then we'll have orgasmic marriages. A sense of accomplishment and satisfaction is experienced knowing you've pleased your woman, yet more importantly, knowing she is completely satisfied. Every marriage has room for improvement. If you think you're an exception, ask your spouse if she or he is completely satisfied. Chances are, they will say they are but after reading this book and applying the concepts to your marriage, you may have a happier spouse.

If you must choose a room in your home to be lazy in, please don't choose the bedroom. The lower dosage of a Viagra tablet is $22.50 – $24.00 per pill and other male enhancing drugs are costly as well. Men will spare no cost to satisfy a woman in the bedroom. Imagine if the male and female placed the same efforts outside the bedroom as they do inside the bedroom. Wow! Talk about an explosion and fusion of two lives.

- A king beheaded a man because a woman pleased him.

- A man worked for 14 years for a woman's hand in marriage all because she pleased him.

- A woman called her husband Lord because he satisfied her.

- A man gave up his kingdom, throne, and wealth all because a woman thrilled him.

- A married woman desired a slave servant and because he would not please or satisfy her lustful sexual desires, she made false accusations of attempted rape which resulted in the young man going to prison.

- Adam lost eternal life, his relationship with God, and paradise because a woman pleased him.

There's a quality inside the soul of all of us that wants to be wholly physically, emotionally, and spiritually satisfied. When the opposite sex massages that quality, it stimulates the brain drawing him or her into a state of exhilaration. To the man and woman who can connect in a thousand different ways, it's paradise - connecting spirits, connecting souls, and connecting sexually is paradisiac.

"Bone of my bone and flesh of my flesh." When a woman pleases a man and a man pleases a woman it is not tit-for-tat, it's having a sincere desire, thirst, and hunger to meet one another's needs. It's more than reciprocating, it is intimacy at its deepest level. It's appreciating, understanding, loving, and touching the core of your spouse. Touching the soul of another person should be one of the definitions of love. One should love and respect the experience of being in love.

The power of these lessons will inspire, motivate, stimulate, and cause you to reevaluate the health of your relationship. These lessons have the power to turn a bad marriage into a good marriage and a good marriage into a great marriage. The wisdom and knowledge acquired here will help you discover how to please your spouse and how your spouse can please you. When a couple masters the art of pleasing one another, the floodgates of emotional, physical, and spiritual intimacy are opened.

This art of pleasing your spouse is not new, it has simply gotten lost in the state of familiarity with your mate. The art is powerful and will thrust your relationship into a magical state which will rekindle and resuscitate the love and closeness you once shared. How? By creating a Garden of Eden in your marriage and in your home.

# Let's Begin The Journey

# ONE

## GOD'S WONDERFUL GIFT

It is necessary to begin our journey in the book of Genesis since we are talking about marriage. There are so many lessons to be learned by focusing on humanity's first couple...Adam and Eve.

God declared that everything He created was good and very good (Gen 1:31). Part of what was good and very good was the creation and formation of the man and the woman. After God finished His creative work (Gen 2: 1-2), Moses began to give us a summary of how God formed Adam and created Eve.

Adam, who was first formed, had no suitable companion, so from the mind and hands of God, He created woman (Gen 2:20-25). God chose her look, the color of her hair, and her eyes and skin color. He chose her figure, the shape of her breasts, thighs, and legs. Yes, he chose everything that made Eve (internally and externally).

God created the woman, gift wrapped her in shamelessness and presented naked Eve to naked Adam. What an unexpected gift! What a wonderful, splendid, glorious, suitable and pleasurable gift. The gift was not the nakedness, for soon enough they both would be covered with sin and shame. The gift was the woman herself - her total being and everything that made her splendid...body, soul, and spirit.

Eve had never seen a man, so when God introduced and presented her to Adam he also introduced and presented Adam to Eve. You see, they were a gift to each other. Most people do not believe in love at first sight, but for Adam that is exactly what happened. Eve's value and worth were soon manifested in the eyes of her husband, Adam, who will set the example and show all men for generations to come just how pleased he was with his gift of companionship.

The creation of the woman is so marvelous that I will boldly declare… *If God made anything better than a woman, it's still in heaven.*

- God gave the very first present, and the present was a woman.

- It's the female body God entrusts life with.

- It's the female body God so marvelously and uniquely made.

- It's the female who has been assigned connection with a man to create oneness.

- It's the female wife God called a "good thing."

- It's the female who Christ styled as his bride (known as the church)

- It was for the female that angels left heaven to never return.

So, I'll say it again, if God made anything better than a woman, it is still in heaven. Thank God for the woman! Let's take a closer look at (Gen 2:23). Adam sees Eve for the first time and he was pleased. Who wouldn't be? She was beautifully crafted by the hands of the Creator. I believe Eve was beautiful because *all* the daughters of Eve are gorgeous.

Eve satisfied, excited, and stirred emotion in Adam that had been lying dormant. Adam then showed his pleasure for the gift and cried out, *"This is bone of my bone and flesh of my flesh, she shall be called woman."* At that point, Adam had literally lost his mind. He lost the mind of being a single man or should I say about being alone? In the state of euphoria, he started talking about leaving loved ones he didn't even have. He said, "Shall a man leave his father and mother and cleave to his wife? If I were standing in the garden with Adam, I would have said, "Wait a minute, you don't even have earthly parents!" Adam's response may have been "Yes, I know, but if I had parents I would leave them for this gift of companionship."

It's very important that I inject this here. Ladies, Adam said for a man to leave his parents, not *forsake* his parents. Yes, leave your parent's home, dependency, your position as a child, and assume the role of head and leader. Cleave to the wife you have chosen. Adam goes on to enlighten us to the fact the husband and wife should be so united that nothing comes between their love - not even their closest ties, father or mother. Husband and wives must maintain the bone and flesh connection!

## Bone: Deep Inner Connection

A couple's growth is connected to each other's growth as well as their strength and their pain. When a couple is connected by the bone, whatever is done to disturb, injure, or hurt your partner's inner being or wound their emotional state, it will also disturb, injure, or hurt your inner being. Whatever it takes to moisten and strengthen your bones it takes the same thing to moisten and strengthen your spouse's bones.

## Flesh: Visible Outer Connection.

Onlookers should be able to see expressions of love between you and your spouse. The love you share for one another should be expressed through mutual looks, touches, kindness, tenderness, devotion, respect, as well as honor.

Sin produces shame; however, Adam and Eve were naked, but not ashamed. Adam and Eve were pure in a holy place and in the presence of their Creator, but there was another reason why they were not ashamed. Eve knew no shame because she knew Adam was pleased with her. He was completely satisfied. Remember, God chose everything about Eve and everything God created was very good. I'll take the liberty to say Adam was the good, Eve was the very good. Likewise, when Eve looked at Adam, Adam knew that Eve was satisfied. She saw him standing tall as a pillar of strength, looking handsome, with the right complexion and the right connection - Adam knew God.

I can hear some of you saying, "Wait a minute! Are you suggesting that I am not supposed to be ashamed of my body or any of my physical imperfections? Are you suggesting I like everything physically about my spouse?" Let me explain. Whether you are a male or female, you may feel your eyes are too close, your nose too big, your hairline is receding, your teeth are crooked, your breasts are sagging, stomach is too flabby, your stretch marks have stretch marks, hips too wide, you laugh and call yourself thunder thighs, plus I won't even mention the cellulite.

Eve was flawless by every standard, but unlike Adam and Eve who were formed and created by the direct hand of God, for us to get to Earth, we had to travel from the male body to the female body, make a connection inside of her, and stay in her hotel until birth. Physically, there are things all of us may not like about ourselves, things we wish we could transform. In this day of cosmetic surgery, many are doing just that. We are our own worst enemies.

People do not always see us the way we see ourselves. It may sound strange, but it is possible for someone to love you and you don't love yourself. It is plausible for one to be satisfied with who you are, and you are not satisfied with yourself. You must not define yourself by your imperfections. The adage is true, "beauty is in the eye of the beholder." What's wrong with you is not who you are.

God gave the gift. Adam accepted the gift. He could have said, "No, thank you," but he didn't. Your companion is not perfect, but they are an irreplaceable gift. The problem with our society is we keep marrying and divorcing bodies. When you marry a person, you do not marry a body per se, you marry a mind. Their thoughts, emotions, beliefs, values, principles, and religion contribute to who they are.

All of us want to look our best, nevertheless, the gift is more important than the wrapping. Our physical body is only the wrapping, the essence is on the inside so although the wrapping helps make the gift appealing, the real value is connecting with what's inside. It may be difficult, but we can feel good because of our interior without allowing our exterior to determine our response to our surroundings.

To further reiterate this point, let me share a personal story with you. My wife is an attractive woman and has always taken pride in her appearance while also being very conscious of her weight. Whenever we are at the beach or a water park, she will bring to my attention the physical contour of another woman's body. As far as my wife is concerned, the woman being observed is usually wearing a bathing suit she *really* shouldn't be wearing. My wife's remarks are in no way intended to belittle or criticize the other woman. What she is insinuating is if this woman can wear a bikini with flaws greater than her own, why is she so self-conscious? As I previously stated, the other woman is not allowing her physique to dictate her response to her surroundings.

## Satisfaction Guaranteed

Imagine going into a restaurant and the atmosphere is, if you are nice, we will be nice. If you are rude, we will be rude. If you disrespect us, we will disrespect you. Well, this is exactly what we do in our relationships. We make our actions contingent upon how our spouse relates to us. This way will always produce friction, anger, resentment, bitterness, sleepless nights, confusion, and tension. In business, it's all about pleasing and satisfying the customer and those in business who don't understand this principle will not be in business long. This same principle should be applied to our relationships. To be heard, one must first hear. To be understood, one must first seek to understand.

Today, so many relationships are all about *me* and what have you done for *me* lately. Physical needs have taken precedence over emotional needs. It's no longer about our spouse's emotional balance. For the sake of marriage, couples are asking each other to transform themselves and to give up who they really are, the very core of their existence. Regardless of what your spouse does or doesn't do, the core of who you are should not be sacrificed to make another person happy. For example, let's assume you are a giver by nature. Giving brings you great joy and you simply delight in helping others. It's who you are! Now, for several reasons, your spouse may have a problem with your generous heart.

To maintain the harmony within the relationship, adjusting or altering a few things you do may be necessary. However, you should not be forced to live your life contrary to your psychological makeup. I'm not talking about right or wrong or good or bad. Pleasing one another is the key to our heart's desires. It is not demanding, insisting, or attempting to control or manipulate one another. It is simply learning how to satisfy their needs. I'm not speaking of some crazed, jealous, controlling, insecure, male or female, or a one-sided love affair.

It's demoralizing pouring your heart into a relationship and getting very little in return. To a certain degree, if a relationship is going to be totally healthy, the scales of love must be balanced. Love must be reciprocated, love must compromise, and love must seek to please. (I Corinthians Chapter 13)

Concerning our shortcomings, each of us must stop searching for a reason to hold on to who we have become. We must strive to become who and what we are not. Simply, the best possible version of one's self. The art of pleasing your spouse is a powerful concept and can alter the events of your life.

**Wives:**

1. How does he like his food?      please him

2. How does he like you to dress for work or church?      compromise

3. How does he feel about you being on time?      please him

**Husband:**

1. How does she like to be spoken to?      please her

2. What does she wish you would do more of?      do it

3. What bad habit does she wish you would get rid of?      eliminate it

There are times when the above is not feasible, but I am suggesting the husband and wife adopt a new way of thinking. If this new way of living is applied, it will slowly transform the marriage from the ordinary to the extraordinary. At first, you may feel a little awkward - feeling one thing on the inside, yet doing something else on the outside. To change the atmosphere of the relationship, the husband and the wife need to maintain this new-found path until it becomes the cornerstone of their marriage.

There was a time you liked everything about your spouse and you would do anything for them. This is the state of mind needed to eliminate negative energy from our relationship. Change should not be made for the sake of changing, but for the betterment of the relationship. If you are already giving a hundred percent in any area of your relationship, then you are giving all you can give; however, if you are only giving fifty percent there is certainly room for growth.

Sometimes giving 100% of what you know is not
giving 100% of everything there is to know.

To reach a harmonious accord, we must continue to expand our thinking, wisdom, and knowledge. God said it is not good for man to be alone, so he gave man a companion. The Creator knows what's best for us. If he said it is not good for man to be alone, it is definitely not good for man to be alone. Nowadays, because of all the pressure on marriages, the single life looks more appealing to some. Couples who have been married for ten, twenty, or thirty years all of a sudden are calling it quits. God's word is true. It is not good for man to be alone. Take notice! A man will get out of one relationship and enter another one. Why is this? It is for companionship. The man and the woman need each other. In marriage, each person brings qualities and traits that will enhance the life of the other.

My brother Alex said to a small group of men and me that if God removed all the women from the face of the Earth he would not want to stay here. Some of the men missed his meaning and thought he wanted to be the only man on the new planet with all those women. That's not what he was saying because one woman is *more* than enough. My brother Alex was simply suggesting that he understands the overwhelming value of the woman and understands she is the most precious, irreplaceable gift on Earth. He was hoping to awaken the consciousness of the men listening. My brother's hope was to stress that a woman is not our footstool or someone to be abused or misused. The woman is God's magnificent, glorious, wonderful, unique gift. If such a thing would happen and God removed all women, you can rest assured knowing if my brother found a way out of here I wouldn't be far behind him. I, like my brother, am truly grateful for the gift of a woman's companionship. More specifically, I'm grateful for my gift, my wife.

I was talking to a friend whose husband died of cancer at the young age of twenty-nine. At the time of his death, they had been married for about a year. What should have been the most exciting time of their life together turned out to be the most challenging and disheartening. At the time, my friend felt fate dealt her a cruel hand. You see, for many years she fervently prayed for companionship. Her prayer was answered, yet his death followed shortly thereafter. She would proclaim, "How could God allow this to happen? Why now? This is not fair!" As I struggled to help her reconcile her faith, I began to empathize with her and feel her pain. She was intensely troubled by the loss of her husband.

As she spoke with me, I learned what so many take for granted. The simple things like having someone to scratch your back, turn the lights on or off, or watch the baby while you run to the store are part of the companionship package. Maybe you need someone to pass you a towel as you enter or exit the shower, or need someone for security reasons in the midnight hour.

There are three hundred twenty-five million people in the United States of America, 7.5 billion worldwide. One of the saddest things for me to hear is someone, regardless of their age, expressing how lonely they are. Not loneliness due to isolation, but loneliness due to feeling no one loves, cares, or understands them. How can this be? In a world that's seemingly over populated, everyone should be able to find that special someone to share life with. Unfortunately, that's not the case. Allow me to shock you with the following statement:

> There is no guarantee in life for marital love - no one has to love you, care for you, or be good to you. The fact that you have found someone to share your life with should generate overwhelming appreciation for him or her.

In this modern day of conveniences, taking your spouse for granted is so easy to do. We have become accustomed to having life's necessities at a moment's notice. To function in today's society, all one needs to do is flip a switch, swipe a card, click a device or speak to it. We are hurried to the point whereby fast food is becoming slow food and all we have to do is drive through. We desire warp speed for computers and the Internet. All these things are good and help make life better; however, I'm convinced if you ever experience total isolation for an extended period of time, you will trade it for some type of human contact. Neither the husband nor the wife desires to be in a relationship feeling like their spouse wants to be out of the marriage. Every couple needs to have their own little special way of relaying they're still in love and if they had to live their life over again, it would be with their chosen bride or their groom. Your companion is a gift from God. Live daily with them as if it were going to be your last day.

When things are really good between my wife and me, I will jokingly comment that I'm going to renew our marriage contract for another year. This is my way of telling her I am satisfied with the love she is providing.

## Key Points

- A companion is a gift from God.

- "Woman" is God's cure for man's loneliness.

- We must honor the choice we made for a mate because God honors our choice.

- For the gift of companionship, joy within the relationship is proof of appreciation.

- Happiness is someone for you to love and someone to love you.

- Pleasing one another is the key to gaining your heart's desires.

# The Journey Continues...

Two

# MAKE YOUR SELECTION

For Adam, God delivered his wife to him, but the rest of us must explore, search, and weed out to find our mate. More likely than not, if you are reading this book you have already made your selection. If you are single, prayer and wisdom will help you get through the selection process. The journey continues.

I have been accused of being old fashioned. If old fashioned means doing things right, well, I guess I'm old fashioned. When it comes to looking for a mate, clearly the male should do the pursuing or as they call it today, the chasing. It's okay and even nicer for the female to leave some breadcrumbs along the way, this adds to the excitement.

Out of all the females on Earth, a man must select one to be his bride. When you think about spending the rest of your life with this one person, the selection process can be tremendous.

- Where do you start?
- What do you look for?
- How will I know she's the one?
- What color, size, or religion?
- How will I know when I am ready?
- What age must I make this selection?
- Who will help me decide?

Females may not fully understand this aspect of what a man is up against; therefore, the male is oftentimes mislabeled. This is understood because men have a problem with a woman's selection process, as well.

In his book, *Act Like A Lady And Think Like A Man*, Steve Harvey talks about his 90-day rule which suggests all women withhold the cookie (sex) for the first 90 days of dating. Although I am a big Steve Harvey fan, I somewhat disagree with the 90-day rule. His message is clear and understandable and although controlling one's sexual behavior for 90 days may not be the *highest* standard, at least his rule is representative of a standard; therefore, my hat's off to Mr. Harvey. Love you, Steve!

I, on the other hand, subscribe to the highest of standards - *leave the cookie in the wrapper until a serious commitment has been made.*

While writing this portion of the book, my mind drifts back to an encounter I had with an over-zealous car salesman. I was visiting my home state of Florida and one day with nothing to do, I made the decision to go car browsing. Dreaming is what dreamers do! You know the drill. While on the lot, I was approached by this car salesman who insisted I locate my vehicle of choice. Unbeknownst to the salesman, I had zero purchasing power and no real plans to buy a car. I was simply LOOKING.

Upon choosing a car, the salesmen retrieved the keys for a test drive. It was a nice test drive. I then confessed to the non-existing funds in my bank account and my low credit score. Simply put, the car salesman was officially informed I could not afford the car. For some unknown reason, his zeal prevented him from hearing my words. This man honestly refused to take no for an answer.

To my shock and dismay, this guy insisted that I keep the car over the weekend. Still attempting to back out of the situation, I told him I was visiting from Texas. He was not swayed. Like a shark to blood, he was laser focused and hungry, and I was his prey. You would think hearing that I lived in another state 524 miles away would make the poor guy stand down. To the contrary, his passion for the sale made him up the offer and he insisted I take the car for a month. Double shock! "Here are the KEYS see you in 30 days."

At the end of the 30 days, someone higher in the car shark food chain called me with a few choice words and requested I return the vehicle to Florida ASAP which I did. Now, to my earth shattering point: This story reflects in similar ways how singles handle the cookie (sex). Although I was powerless to make the purchase, the over-zealous car salesman *willingly* handed me the keys.

Ladies, to your own detriment, you keep passing out the cookie to men who have no desire to purchase or to marry. You are going too deep, too fast. Selecting a mate is not like choosing a car's make, model, and color. It would be easier and less time consuming if all we had to consider was age, color, and size when choosing a mate. Every woman

> Place a value on yourself as well as the cookie.

should feel special knowing her man had a choice and he chose you. It's sad, but true - not every woman will hear those life changing words, *"Will you marry me?"*

The following list was specifically designed with singles in mind. A man's approach to this list will be from the bottom to the top (ascending). More times than not, a man's focus is on #35 along with Marvin Gaye's hit song, *Let's Get It On.* It is not a man's nature to turn down sex, so if offered he will most likely accept without any intentions of any type of return.

Ladies, you must approach this list in a descending order. The passage of time (years) should determine the depth of your sharing or the exposure of your soul. This list may not guarantee you a husband, but it will keep you from being another notch on some man's belt. These are questions every single woman should ask her potential suitor. More importantly, the answers to the questions should be pondered deeply. His answers should be compared to your portrait of a relationship. Like a puzzle, each answer is a piece of the puzzle to unlock the core of your potential mate:

1. Are you a natural born leader or are you a follower?
2. What do you dream (prosperity) about?
3. Are you an introvert or an extrovert?
4. What is it about you that I don't know, but should know?
5. Do you have a college degree?
6. Are you currently employed? If so, where?
7. How many jobs have you held in the last five or ten years?
8. What's your highest credit score?
9. What are your short-term goals?
10. What are your long-term goals?
11. Do you have a budget or are you winging it each month?
12. What investment firm are you with?
13. Where do you invest your money?
14. Tell me about your faith/belief system?
15. What are some of your double standards?
16. What books have you read?
17. Who's your hero and why?
18. Who's your mentor?
19. How many children do you have?
20. How many mothers between all your children?
21. Do you have a criminal record?
22. What are your thoughts concerning domestic violence?
23. What's your illegal drug of choice?

24. What is your HIV status?

25. How long was your longest relationship?

26. What caused your previous relationship to end?

27. Do you have hopes of settling down one day?

28. Do you see marriage in your near future?

29. When you get married how many children would you like to have?

30. Describe your ideal woman.

31. What attracted you to me?

32. Do you know the difference between love and lust?

33. Have you ever had a sexual encounter with the same sex?

34. How young/old is too young/old for you to date, marry, or romance?

35. Do you believe in premarital sex?

36. What makes you the one for me?

37. Can you truthfully say that you are a one-woman man?

38. How will you honor me in marriage?

39. Do you believe in pre-nuptial agreements? Why or why not?

40. Other than infidelity, what's your marital deal breaker?

41. How many times a week should a married couple have sex?

42. Tell me about your ultimate sexual fantasy?

43. What's your family generational curse?

44. What sickness or disease does your family have a history of?

45. Describe your parent's relationship.

46. Are you striving to be like your father (in marriage) or better than your father?

47. Other than vaginal intercourse, what type of sex have you been exposed to?

48. Do you find oral sex to be distasteful, repulsive, intolerable or delightful?

49. Do you have a desire, craving, or yearning for anal sex with your future wife?

50. Do you consider sex toys in the bedroom taboo?

The complexity of the process of choosing a mate is so serious and enormous that some men are frightened away from selecting; however, with confidence, wisdom, knowledge, and an understanding of yourself and the opposite sex, you can select. I don't think she realized it at the time, but my mother helped shape my views, at an early age, for selecting a wife. Her advice came not in many words, yet impacted my life in a powerful way. Her words still ring loud and true in my mind as if she spoke them yesterday. On a warm, summer day in a sincere voice she spoke, "Ed don't let just anybody have your children." It wasn't a heavy or deep statement, but it hit me like a ton of bricks. I heard her words, but most of all I received her message and it was this:

- Your children's mother must be a special person to/for you.

- Don't be sleeping around, you may impregnate someone you did not intend to.

- Know the woman you are intimate with.

- Maintain high standards for yourself.

- There are consequences to not having high standards.

Those were and are valuable lessons for a sixteen-year-old. I don't recommend, encourage, or approve marrying so young, but here is my story: I was twenty-one and she was seventeen when we exchanged vows. We met at church which certainly was a plus for me. For the most part, we were raised up together. We started out as friends, nothing more, and nothing less. After a while, I found myself developing feelings for her. I got the courage to make my feelings known. It wasn't easy letting her know I was interested. What age was she? She was sixteen. Okay… she was fifteen.

With a strong religious upbringing, all we could do was talk, which is part of what prompted us to marry when we did. Her name was Cynthia Ann Young, and she was beautiful and still is today. I was hooked. I was attracted to her innocence. She was pristine and full of life. We would talk for hours and hours sharing our innermost secrets. We were both good listeners and communication allowed our bond to grow stronger by the day. The more she listened the more connected I became and the deeper I found myself sinking. As a young man, I was full of dreams. Although I had not yet accomplished anything meaningful, I had a vision and Cynthia believed in me.

Looking back, our communication was our sex and was the bond that held our young relationship together. Even at my young age, I knew I wanted to marry a woman with high morals, values, principles, intelligence, and someone respectful. Most of all, I wanted to marry someone with strong religious convictions. My mind was made up at an early age. I'd found in Cynthia everything I wanted in a woman. I was going to make her my wife and thirty-seven years later here we are. She is still the love of my life and she completes me. By the way, I can truthfully say she is the mother of all my children Katrina and Meagan (twins), who are twenty-eight, and Erica (baby girl) who is twenty-four. Thank you, Momma, for helping me choose my bride.

Proverb 18:22
   *"He that finds a wife finds a good thing.*

When a married man views his wife as a good thing the relationship is at least on the right track. When a man is given the gift of companionship, his mate is to be appreciated, loved, honored, treasured, respected and protected. That is what you do with gifts, isn't it?

Because of problems and disagreements, many couples will say God did not give them their mate; therefore, they are not a gift. This long held view is wrong. God does not choose our mate for us, but He honors the choice we make. Eve caused Adam some serious problems, but she was still his glorious gift.

One of the most amazing and astonishing occurrences of a woman pleasing a man took place in the Garden of Eden. In (Genesis 3:6) Adam finds himself in a dilemma. Eve had been deceived, eaten the forbidden fruit, and presented it to him to partake. God's word flooded his mind, *"Of every tree of the garden thou may freely eat, but of the tree of good and evil thou may not eat."* Adam looked at Eve – the woman who pleases him. He hears the word of God, which should direct him, yet Adam is confused about what to do.

Adam found himself positioned to please God or to please Eve. We know the story. Adam ate the fruit. The amazing thing is Adam was not deceived. Adam ate the fruit because Eve pleased him.

1 Timothy 2:14

*"And Adam was not deceived, but the woman being deceived was in the transgression."*

Am I saying, if given the choice, a man should choose his wife over the Creator? Absolutely not! The case I am making is if Eve can please Adam to the point of causing him to disobey the commandments of God, your mate can be pleased into fulfilling the righteous desires of your heart. Adam and Eve prove that mastering the art of pleasing your spouse will not only allow a couple to snore together, but they will soar together, or in this case face their demise together. Because Adam was pleased *with* Eve, he wanted to please her. Women may desire to pray, "Lord, give my husband the spirit of Adam," but a better prayer is, "Lord, let true love be the epitome of our union."

Eve caused Adam to lose:

- His relationship with the Creator
- Eternal life
- Paradise

Why would Adam give up eternal life in paradise with his Creator? He did not give up eternal life in the sense he did not want it any more. He merely surrendered to the emotional influence Eve had over him. Adam may have been strong, but Eve's power or the power of her love was stronger. Adam may have been a conqueror, but Eve was an authority - the woman of the house. It may be hard to believe that Adam gave up paradise for a woman and you may be thinking there just had to be another reason...maybe it was the fruit.

Stop and think: If a monkey brought the forbidden fruit to Adam, do you think he would have eaten it? Same tree, same fruit! It was not about the tree, nor the fruit. It was about the woman. The male/female relationship should be secondary to their relationship with the Creator. You and I can question what Adam did, but it will not change the events of that day.

> *The weak routinely surrenders to the strong.*

Marriage is about finding the right person, but more importantly, it's about being the right person for the one you have found. It is true, *"Mr. Right is looking for Mrs. Right."* I have heard men refer to their wives as being stupid or ignorant. I remind them their wife is clearly not the one who is delinquent. The Bible says, "He that finds a wife, finds a good thing." Not only should you marry one woman, you should be a one-woman man. The same can be expressed about the woman, not only should you marry one man, you should be a one-man woman.

1 Corinthians 7:33-34

*"A married man should seek the things that please his wife. A married woman should seek the things that please her husband."*

Physical, emotional, and spiritual intimacy allows us to learn a person inside and out. The knowledge we have of one another should be used for the betterment and not the detriment of the relationship. If you know your husband is time conscience, he's not interested in your excuses. Your attitude should reflect your attempt to be on time. *That's pleasing.* If it infuriates your wife when you raise your voice, your attitude should display watching your tone and not raise your voice. *That's pleasing.* A life of mutual respect, love, and affirmation will produce a state of wholeness and wellness. By trying to accomplish this, both husband and wife will feel complete in the relationship. Just as sperm and egg unite to produce a human life, so it is with a husband and wife. Oneness can only occur when they are connected to the spirit of each other.

Loving your spouse means loving yourself

- I should speak to her as if I am speaking to myself.
- When I love her, I am loving myself.
- When I hold her, I am giving her what I need.
- When I care for her, I am caring for myself.
- Because I forgive myself, I forgive him.

When a man finally takes a woman's hand in marriage, he is announcing to the world, "I have made my choice. I have sorted through all the precious stones, emeralds and rubies and found a diamond." He is announcing to the human race, "Of all the precious jewels, her sparkle out shines them all." What was it about her that made you ask for her hand in marriage? What was it about him that made you accept his proposal? Your answer to these questions should be the very thing you strive to hold on to.

All of us have made purchases and immediately developed a strong case of buyer's regret and for whatever reason we felt the urge to return the item. Most return policies are simple and allow us to exchange an item or get a full refund. God has a return policy as well, but it's not like the most common ones we hear about today. For example, most of the remarks we hear about marriage are: this isn't working out, irreconcilable differences, we grew apart, I wasn't ready, he/she wasn't the one for me, and so on.

In the eyes of God, once a man makes his selection for a wife, the choice is for life. The only way out is through death or a violation of the marriage covenant. God's return policy is not to return the spouse back to their Maker. Of course, there are Christians and non-Christians alike who would love to do just that; however, if a violation of the marital covenant were to occur, God's return policy is to return them to their former state of singleness, if one so desires.

Some men will introduce or present their wife as their better half. For some reason, I have always resisted introducing my wife in this manner. My thinking is, if she is the better half, then that makes me the worse half. I have never considered myself the worse part of my marriage and pride myself on knowing how to love and respect my wife. After pondering the statement more, I now understand why some men will voice this distinction. A man who truly feels his wife is his better half does so because of their history as a couple. This man's success, freedom, peace of mind, salvation, wellness, and even his life is all because of his woman's strength and contribution. A man who proclaims his wife as his better half understands that choice of this woman has made his life what it is today.

## Married Life vs Single Life

Both have their advantages as well as disadvantages. To marry or not to marry depends on which set of advantages and which set of disadvantages one prefers. If you enjoy having someone to share every aspect of life with, then marriage is for you. To the contrary, if you enjoy being alone, accountable to no one, self-centered or afraid of commitment, you are not ready for a commitment to marriage. The choice to marry or not marry is an individual decision every man and woman must choose for themselves.

## Key Points

- Knowing yourself and what you really want in a mate will make the selection process much easier. Every man needs to know when to end his search for a potential spouse.

- He that finds a wife finds a good thing.

- When a married man views his wife as a good thing, the relationship is at least on the right track. When a man is given the gift of companionship, his mate is to be appreciated, loved, honored, treasured, respected, and protected.

- The married man should seek the things that please his wife, and the married woman should seek the things that please her husband.

- Your mate can be pleased into fulfilling the righteous desires of your heart.

- Marriage is a lifetime commitment.

# The Journey Continues...

# Three

# MAKE A BABY

> The latter part of Genesis Chapter 3 shares how
> Adam and Eve are driven out of the Garden of Eden.
> Adam and Eve have lost everything…except each
> other.

Genesis 3: 23-24

*"Therefore the Lord God sent him forth from the Garden of Eden to till the ground from whence he was taken. So, he drove out the man; and placed at the east of the Garden of Eden Cherubims, and a flaming sword; which turned every way to keep the way of the tree of life." Chapter 4 begins with Eve giving birth to two sons.*

Genesis 4: 1-2

*"And Adam knew Eve his wife; and she conceived, and bare Cain, and said, I have gotten a man from the Lord. And she again bares his brother Abel. And Abel was a keeper of sheep, but Cain was a tiller of the ground."*

As chapter three ends and chapter four begins, there's a problem. From an individual perspective, Adam should be angry and upset with Eve, but he isn't. Come on, this woman played a significant role in him losing his home, relationship with the Creator, and eternal life. After years of studying human behavior, it's safe for me to say that if we were Adam and Eve, Chapter 4 from the King James Version of the Bible would not read as it does. As a matter of fact, if the best couple you know were Adam and Eve, the chapter would not read as it does.

Let's recreate the final scenes of Chapter 3 after Adam and Eve have eaten the forbidden fruit. (Genesis 3:24) God said to them, "Get your things and get out." If a couple of today were Adam and Eve, Chapter 4 would begin similarly to what I have written below. Indulge me if you will.

Chapter 4: 1- 12

We'll call this version
*The Common Man's Up-to-Date Bible*

1. *God has kicked us out of the garden. I have lost everything. Adam says to Eve, I need to speak with you.*
2. *I can't believe what you have done. You had no business talking to the serpent. Why didn't you let me handle it?*
3. *Because of you I have lost everything. I wish I had never met you. You are so very, very stupid.*
4. *Eve says to Adam, I am sorry, Adam says you are right about that. You are sorry. Don't touch me, says Adam. I am going to bed, so he turns his back to her and attempts to go to sleep. Still steaming, he jumps out of bed shouting, I can't believe you did that!*
5. *Adam attacks Eve verbally. If they put your brain in a bird the*

*bird would fly backwards. If they put it in a parrot, instead of the parrot saying Polly wants a cracker, it will say cracker wants a Polly.*

6. *Why in the world did I name you Eve? I should have named you Grieve because that's all you have done is grieved me. What I should do is knock the taste out of your month.*

7. *I want out of this marriage, I want a divorce. It's over, do you hear me? It's over. Pack your bags. I am taking you back to your daddy.*

Allow me to take this a little further since anger produces anger and harsh words stir up wrath. Adam's tongue has stirred Eve up. Let's continue this chapter.

8. *Eve says wait a minute buddy, you were in the garden before I was. You knew what the Creator said. Don't blame me for what you did.*

9. *You are the leader. I didn't force the fruit down your throat. And anyway, who are you calling stupid? You are the one that's stupid. You named all the animals, right? You could have given that happy, hairy, jumping, thing a better name than monkey.*

10. *Monkey, donkey. Boy, you must have stayed up all night long coming up with those names. Man, I wish you would put your hands on me. I'll just shut up! Stop talking to me.*

11. *Eve is upset, hurting, crying, frightened, and feeling very lonely. She is distant and withdrawn.*

12. *Eve says to Adam, Adam the pastor says... Adam abruptly interrupts, I don't care what the Pastor, the Supreme Court, the President or Dr. Phil, says. Eve jumps up screaming at the top of her lungs, don't you say nothing about Dr. Phil!*

Sound familiar? Of course, it does. As human beings, our natural inclination is to be angry or upset when we face problems or trouble caused by someone else.

Adam has every right to be angry and upset with Eve. He also has a right to be upset with the punishment, but let's take a real close look at what he does. Stop reading now and turn back to page 39, and read both scriptures again. Can you see it? It's there. Look very closely. Resume reading to see if you discovered the all-important message. Adam goes and makes a baby. Not just one baby, but two.

## What Is The Message Here?

Adam gives us a strong lesson on how to relate to our mate during troublesome times. His spouse messed up, she ruined his life, created unnecessary suffering, usurped authority, and passed the blame. After all of this, Adam (Genesis 4) is having sexual intercourse with Eve. Let me reword that. Adam is making love to Eve. He's kissing, holding, caressing and romancing his wife. He's speaking softly and tenderly expressing his love for the woman God created just for him. Trouble did not change his love or remove the joy he felt when he first laid eyes on Eve. The trouble did not extinguish the overwhelming appreciation and gratitude for Eve being in his life.

It is clearly a choice to express love in times like these. Adam made a choice. A choice that nothing would come between him and Eve - not even anger. Adam did not allow what happened in the Garden of Eden to sever the bond he shared with Eve. Adam realized Eve made an honest mistake. He knew Eve did not purposely set out to hurt him. All of us can make mistakes, *if* it is truly a mistake. See it for what it is. Adam's position was: We'll get through this together - what's done is done - the Creator judged us, and we will accept it and move on.

Can you imagine how awful Eve must have felt? Yes, she felt terrible. I can imagine her standing before Adam repentantly saying, "I am sorry. Take me, hold me, love me, forgive me." Eve wanted and needed to feel secure in Adam's love. She wanted his protection and not his rejection. At that moment, she needed Adam more than ever.

## Facing Trouble In Relationships

When we face problems, ninety percent of the time someone else is to blame. More times than not, we blame our spouse. That's just the way it is. It has been proven that trouble has a way of distressing our health. Problems have the capability to increase our stress level and blood pressure. An increased heart rate and an array of other health issues may occur. Our health benefits when we learn how to let off steam without finding fault, criticizing, condemning, or closing the spirit of our mate, which means your spouse has checked out on you and they are no longer responding to you.

Here's the problem. We become resentful and hostile toward the one's we supposedly love the most. The peace and closeness of our relationship vanish when problems aren't confronted and handled sensitively. The home feels like a battlefield and the husband and wife are launching bombs and hand grenades ripping each other apart unmercifully in an environment filled with tension and dissension. For a brief period, each withdraws only to reload, and attack again. Instead of the rewritten version of Genesis Chapter 4, I am grateful Adam left us a beautiful road map to follow during difficult times.

From the beginning to the end of your marriage, you are going to face problems. Each couple should have a strategic plan of action prepared and in place for these times. One of the things I strongly recommend is a cooling off period. Go for a walk, take a short drive, think about your response, your reaction, and the message you intend to convey. A cooling off period will prevent the two of you from saying or doing things you may regret for the rest of your life. Depending upon what has occurred, or before the matter is resolved, you may need several cooling off periods. Once the two of you reunite, take the time to express the sentiments of your hearts with an open mind and an ear to hear each other's words in the most loving and compassionate way possible.

If you picture your relationship as a patient in a hospital with the two of you as the tending medical physicians, you'll get past the problem much faster. As the relationship specialist, it is necessary to provide the patient with the best care possible. As specialists, the things you say and do should promote healing, mending, or aid in the recovery of the patient. At all costs, efforts should be made to save the life of the patient. Once the patient's health has been restored, the patient will be able to function as healthy people do.

A relationship may progress several years without any adverse circumstances, but this does not mean the relationship is exempt from adversity. Expressing love and support amid pain should be the couple's number one concern when either or is hurting. In marriage, each of us will face hardship. Our greatest lessons will be learned during adversity. Not only lessons about our spouse, but lessons about ourselves as well. It is disturbing to discover, after several years of marriage, the person you thought you knew, you really didn't know.

The crisis Adam and Eve experienced came early in their marriage. In life, there are times when sooner is truly better than later. Difficulties within a marriage can increase one's faith and confidence in the other's ability to lead. It can also further strengthen the marital bond. During difficult times, it is necessary to communicate with

> Without a cooling off period, you may need an ambulance and/or a priest.

your actions as well as your words. With everything in us, we need to fight our natural proclivities and communicate love even when we don't feel loving, and care when we think we couldn't care less.

The husband or wife may have wrecked the car or made a bad investment which caused you to lose money – go make a baby. Adam and Eve certainly did. You may or may not want a baby or maybe you've passed the child rearing stage. Go make a baby is simply my way of saying to be physically intimate with your mate. When you go make a baby during a difficult time, you're saying I love you - what happened has happened - all is well - our union is still strong. It is showing your mate they are valuable and dear to you. So, the next time you face trouble, or a serious problem occurs in your marriage, go make a baby and watch the sparks fly.

As the wounded spouse releases their anger, it will open the spirit of the one that inflicted the wound. Both souls are open for a soothing touch and making love expresses closeness and strengthens the marital bond.

Making love during disappointments or pain is sheer ecstasy. Your greatest lovemaking will occur during these times. Once again, although sex is a private matter between a man and his wife, the activities within their bedroom are still govern by the word of God. When it comes to the sexual practices of the bedroom, this scripture should be used as a guide and not as crutch for unrighteous acts.

Hebrews 13:4
*"Marriage is honorable in all, and the bed undefiled........"*

We cannot use this scripture to justify inordinate (lacking restraint) passion. With that said, it is paramount that all supposed liberties and sexual practices be rooted and grounded in the word. This will be addressed further in the next chapter.

## Key Points

- Couples must work through their anger and frustration. In the midst of difficult times is where genuine love is shown for each other.

- Your spouse needs you to reinforce your love, commitment, as well as closeness. They need your help feeling secure in your love and in the marriage.

- In difficult times, hold each other. Be tender, warm, loving, understanding, and invite each other into your space; your spouse needs this badly.

- Send a strong message to your spouse saying you are going to love them through the good and the bad, rain or sunshine, for better or worse.

- Overall, in the midst of anger, your spouse needs to know you are still pleased with them.

- Learn to provide guidance and instruction for the mishap without making your spouse feel they are the mishap. Voice displeasure for the catastrophe, not the individual.

# The Journey Continues...

# Four

## INTIMATE TIME

> Your bedroom should be your Garden of Eden. Exhibit the lessons learned from Adam and Eve. The greatest experience of intimacy will be encountered in the holy righteous state of marriage.

In Adam's day there was no such thing as (IVF) in virtro fertilization. After being kicked out of the garden, Adam and Eve had sexual intercourse. They certainly had to have sex to produce children; however, this was not when they discovered sex. There was romance in the Garden of Eden before the serpent or the fruit. Before the shame and the blame, they understood physical intimacy. The Creator did not give them a manual on lovemaking nor was one necessary. You may be thinking Adam and Eve did not have the intelligence or the desire to participate in such pleasurable acts. Sorry, you're wrong! If Adam is intelligent enough to name all the animals and name Eve, certainly he's capable of understanding what to do with the woman that captivated his mind. The *naked* woman that stood in front of him, I might add.

Genesis 2:19-20

*"And out of the ground the Lord God formed every beast of the field, and every fowl of the air; and brought them unto Adam to see what he would call them: and whatsoever Adam called every living creature that was the name thereof. And Adam gave names to all cattle, and to the fowl of the air, and to every beast of the field; but for Adam there was not found a help meet for him."*

# God Leaves The Garden

The serpent would not have had the opportunity to trick Eve if God was there. Adam would not have eaten the fruit with God present. Children wait until they're away from their parents to misbehave. Adam and Eve were no exceptions.

There are two reasons why God left the Garden. The first reason was he had to take care of some God business. The second reason was so Adam and Eve could be intimate with each other. Sex is a private matter between a husband and wife. God's manifested presence was in the Garden; therefore, God removed Himself, so Adam and Eve could have some personal, one-on-one time.

## Adam and Eve's Wedding Night

Don't get deep on me! Allow me to borrow your mind. Since it's not recorded in the scriptures, one should not concur that Adam and Eve did not have a wedding night. At some point in the Garden, God pronounced Adam and Eve husband and wife, so their first night together was their wedding night.

## The Five Senses of Romance

After the wedding ceremony ended, the only guest has left, and the moon dimmed its light, Adam and Eve slipped into their love chamber already dressed for the occasion. The birds were singing (*sound*), fragrances from the many flowers filled the air (*smell*), Eve is dripping in femininity, radiant, and simply gorgeous (*sight*), Adam runs his finger through Eve's hair and with a special lotion from the Garden, he massages her whole body as they both delight in this new experience (*touch*). Close by, Adam has prepared a basket of fruit, nuts, and berries, which he slowly feeds to Eve as she sips on some freshly squeezed sparkling juice (*taste*).

The conversation has been stimulating and the night exhilarating. As they lay side by side, Adam and Eve engage in giving and receiving pleasure. Since love feels good, this scene will repeat itself time and time again. I don't believe Adam was barbaric in his approach to lovemaking. I don't believe he mounted Eve like a stallion mounts a mare. Perhaps Adam would say to Eve, "Eve, would you like to be fruitful (make love)?" "Yes, Adam, I would like to be fruitful (make love)," Eve would reply. I believe Adam and Eve experienced absolute delight in the arms of one another as passion flooded their souls. Join me in looking at four areas of intimacy that are essential to your relationship.

## Emotional Intimacy

In 2004, Pensacola, Florida experienced one of its worst natural disasters in history. Without a welcoming committee, Hurricane Ivan came to town. Electrical power was lost which left no air conditioning, refrigeration, warm baths, or television. There were thousands of homes destroyed. Trees were down throughout the county. The area looked like a war zone. There were extended gas lines and people were living in total devastation. Living ceased and surviving began.

Imagine if your spouse is emotionally experiencing Ivan-like conditions. Ivan has invaded their day, week, month, or year and they're living with distrust, suspicion, lies, anger, coldness, rejection, harshness, complaints, unfaithfulness, and jealousy. My friend, when this happens physical intimacy is dead. Quoting scriptures will not melt away the enormous iceberg between the two of you.

## Spiritual Intimacy

Most people have a religion, but I am not talking about a religion. I'm talking about a strong belief system. Husbands and wives often share common beliefs about God, fasting, prayer, and worship.

More importantly, worshipping together is essential. The husband who is called to be the priest of his home has a responsibility to ensure false doctrine does not enter the union. Adam, in his failure to protect Eve in the garden allowed the false words of the enemy to break their union with God. The scripture says a house divided against itself cannot stand.

A house divided can lead to:

1. Division/divorce

2. Sexual temptation

3. Cause onlookers to question the strength of the marriage

4. Gives space to the enemy.

The Bible warns against being unequally yoked. I believe a husband and wife in different religions is a portal for divorce.

## Intellectual Intimacy

Intellectual intimacy is sharing ideas and talking to each other. Exchanging points of views, values, and outlooks on life. It's talking through the little things as well as the big things.

## Physical Intimacy

It is a sexual expression which is an indispensable part of your relationship. Couples should make time or better yet, set time for lovemaking. I'll deal more with this later.

---

Spiritual Intimacy Creates Emotional Intimacy.

Lack of Emotional Intimacy Kills Physical Intimacy.

Emotional Intimacy Creates Physical Intimacy.

---

## Now Let's Really Talk

1 Corinthians 7:3-5

*"Let the husband render unto the wife due benevolence: and likewise also the wife unto the husband. The wife hath not power of her own body, but the husband: and likewise also the husband hath not power of his own body, but the wife. Defraud ye not one another, except it be with consent for a time, that ye may give yourselves to fasting and prayer; and come again, that Satan tempt you not for your incontinency."*

1 Corinthians 7: 33-34

*"But he that is married careth for the things that are of the world, how he may please his wife. There is   difference also between a wife and a virgin. The unmarried woman careth for the things of the Lord, that she may be holy both in body and in spirit: But she that is married careth for the things of the world, how she may please her husband."*

Married couples ought to have regular sexual relations. It is your duty to fulfill the sexual needs of your spouse. When you offer yourself in a sexual manner you're not doing them a favor; it's a mutual obligation. To the wife, when it comes to sex, your body is not your body, but your husband's body. Also, the husband's body is not his body, but the wife's body. It is clear the husband and the wife have a right to each other's body just like you have a right to air. Husbands and wives have exclusive possession in this area. Do not deprive each other in the exercising of this God-given right. It is your job to satisfy your mate's needs. You are the fireman when their sexual flames erupt. It is your emergency - your emergency alone to extinguish the flames and quench the heat of their passion. If left unattended you will be giving space to another, if only in the mind. We must be honest with each other. Sexual immorality is as prevalent in the house of worship as it is outside of it.

Somehow couples have allowed circumstances to suffocate their relationship. Love, passion, care, and concern are all being affected as they struggle to turn a house into a home. Because of stifling conditions within the marriage, one or both becomes convinced their needs can no longer be met by the other. It's crucial for husbands and wives to seek the things that please each other. This is the way it was designed to be; however, we must face the truth about the state of most marriages. The union is suffering because we've gotten away from the mindset to meet each other's needs.

Since it is used repeatedly in this book, I want to focus a little more attention on the word, *please*. To gratify your mate, I am not suggesting that either party does anything that violates their conscience or beliefs. During the question and answer section of my marriage seminars, I regularly receive the following questions or statements.

- What is off limits in the bedroom?
- Doesn't the Bible say the married bed is undefiled?
- What goes on in our bedroom is no one else's business.
- If I don't satisfy my spouse, someone else will.
- If it feels good what is wrong with it?
- Regardless of what it is, should I please my spouse?

I am very careful how I answer such questions. First and foremost, sex is a private matter between a man and his wife. Secondly, each of us interprets and expresses our Christian liberties differently. Thirdly, you have a trusted pastor, counsel, or knowledgeable friend that can assist you with discovering what is permissible and what is not.

Pleasing one another should be secondary to pleasing God. Nonetheless, there are times when a husband or wife's desires conflict with the others' belief or comfort zone. Regardless of the reason, if they're uncomfortable with a certain act or position, the selfish response will be, "get over it." We must become better communicators. God gave us the sanctity of marriage; therefore, His word should be our guide concerning these most delicate matters. After an indebt study of His word, both parties must submit themselves to the word of God and both must be open to the request or practice. Still, a sexual desire must *not* cross the lines of purity, decency, or righteousness.

If there is a psychological barrier that's preventing one or the other from fully committing or participating sexually, coercion is not needed, but patience, understanding, and possibly counseling is. There are some women who practice lovemaking partially clothed and I'm not talking about clothed in sexy lingerie. If something like this is causing harm in your marriage, take a serious look at your part in the relationship.

> No one should be asked to do anything they consider repulsive.

You do not want to constantly pour water on your spouse's fire. Ask yourself if you should please them or please yourself. Consider what should be done when pleasing one is humiliating to the other. To answer these questions, we must treat our spouse the way we want to be treated. There are sexual acts that all of us will find repugnant. Love should be freely expressed. Coercion has no place in the bedroom.

Ephesians 5:28-29

*"So ought men to love their wives as their own bodies he that loveth his wife loveth himself. For no man ever yet hated his own flesh; but nourisheth and cherisheth it, even as the Lord the church."*

When the sexual desires of a husband or wife conflict with the other, the proper response for the husband or the wife should be, "Honey, I love you enough to not ask you to do anything you find offensive." One rule of thumb to help couples get over these sexual hurdles is to first please your mate, mentally, then seek to please them physically. Ask your spouse what their desires are. Once this has been established, one should conduct themselves accordingly. For certain decisions, husband and wife both need to understand it is not your place to agree or disagree, it is your duty to respect the decision of your mate. Stop trying to have a say so in every aspect of their life. Individual preferences should not be trodden over to satisfy the sexual desires of either party. Pleasing your mate should be a lifestyle. A lifestyle that expresses being there for your spouse to make their life better.

## Time For Romance

Husband and wife require quality time with each other. Create a love chamber to be a special place where the two of you relax, share and retire for physical intimacy. Year after year, the square footage of homes continues to increase. Have a purpose for each room in your home. Have a room for discussing serious problems, watching television and entertaining. There is a time and a place for all things. In your home, you clearly need a time and a place to converse the matters of your heart.

Couples should strive to protect the atmosphere of their love chamber. Your bedroom should be for the two of you. Your love chamber should be a place associated with love, joy, happiness, and closeness. Animosity, ill feeling, or bitterness has no place in this room. If you fail to maintain the ambiance of your bedroom, unsuitable topics will continuously rise during conversations. Talk that produces instantaneous anger, guilt, regret or shame should not be discussed. If this occurs, negative feelings will surface, eroding the intimacy between the two you. Regardless of your reason for bringing up the undesirable, I assure you it will not generate the response you were seeking. More times than not, it will produce an argument and destroy any real chance of closeness.

Even if physical intimacy is not going to take place, couples should retire for the evening, listening to the concerns of each other. Topics shared should be expressed in a loving way and the things heard received in the spirit of love. Three to four times a week, husbands and wives need to go to bed at the same time. This act demonstrates to your mate, they are a priority. This time is for the two of you to really connect with each other. The ringer should be turned off with all calls placed on hold. A good conversation starter is to inquire about their day. In other words, you're saying you're interested in their feelings and how they feel about the events of the day. As you listen to your spouse, listen to detect what is needed, if anything. I am a strong believer of closing each day in unity and beginning each new day in unity.

My wife loves me to massage her body, yet after giving her a full body massage we sometimes manage to end up in a verbal dispute. I've noticed when I massage her psyche and her self-worth, the night turns out differently. Why is this? It's because her spirit is open...love is in the air. Of course, nothing is done to manipulate or to control the evening's events.

With modern technology, we can create an atmosphere that expresses love in an utmost way. Since men are visual, lovemaking should not only be scheduled, but it should be planned. This is a special time for the two of you. Before a wife presents herself to her husband, she should adorn and beautify herself. After a shower or bubble bath, his favorite perfume, body oil, along with that special attire, you are now ready for the grand entrance. When the wife beautifies herself, it's part of the excitement for the man plus it adds to his inquisitiveness, creating anticipation for the turn of events about to occur. The wife must willingly present herself. Her body language should say take me, I'm yours, I am here for your delight. She must connect with her touch, kiss, embrace, and the tenderness of the moment.

Her words must match her body language. If the words are saying take me, and the body language is saying, let's get this over with, he will receive both messages. Depending on his mood or needs, he will either complete the act for self-gratification only or he will terminate the act altogether. News Flash! I mentioned earlier that it's not a man's nature to turn down sex; however, there are times that they do.

## Cold Sex Not Hot Sex!

Men need to be mindful that the romantic climate of their love chamber is not the responsibility of the woman alone. It is equally important for husbands to voluntarily participate in creating a pleasant environment. Soft music and candles are not the starting point. Proper grooming will be a much better place to begin. Once a woman presents herself to her husband, conveying the message that he is satisfied with the presentation is important. As she offers herself to him, he receives her without inhibiting her. It is vital for the husband to receive his wife as a gift. He should let her know that he is satisfied as well as appreciative of the gift of her companionship.

As a part of the woman's preparation for presenting herself, she must pull, tuck, arch, hide, cut, clip, nip, rub, comb, brush, rinse, and spray before the process is complete. Likewise, men cannot expect the wife to beautify and then justify his failure to properly groom himself. Proper grooming is essential. Allow your spouse to instruct you concerning what is pleasurable and what is not. Be receptive to feedback by initiating the following: show me how you would like to be touched - show me what I am doing right or wrong - explain what is pleasing or what's painful for you.

Intimacy does not begin with the act of sexual intercourse, nor does it end with sexual intercourse. During sexual relations, husband and wife will bring about one of the greatest feelings on earth. Through sexual exhilaration, the couple will take each other to the mountaintop, but lovemaking is not over at this point. You should continue to passionately hold and caress each other until both descend this sexual high. You went to the mountaintop together, so you must come down this mountain high together. When you continue to be affectionate, your mate will know it wasn't all about you, but it was about them as well. By doing this, you will send a strong message with wonderful ramifications.

Couples must maintain their energy level when it comes to lovemaking. Lovemaking requires effort and the husband and wife cannot come to bed totally depleted expecting to satisfy the needs of the other. Fatigue will invade and rob you of the moment. A lazy lover is not a smart lover. Energy is needed for your nights as well as your days. Your mental and physical response will become lackadaisical without energy and you'll be simply going through the motions! There are times when a hundred percent is not yours to give. That is understandable; however, the routine of only giving thirty percent must go. Do not make continual excuses for being tired or fall into a groove of sluggish lovemaking.

Because of the daily demands of a woman, it's expected for her body to be tired quite often. A man won't complain about self-service sex and although he may participate in such activity, this should not become a substitute for the wife fully giving herself to her husband. There are times when a man desires his wife in the worst way. Because men interpret love as sex, and sex as love, it's important that the wife understands this. Love for him is interpreted as you are there physically, emotionally, and lively. When a man desires love instead of sex, he can pull up to your self-service lifeless body, serve himself and be angry afterwards. He became angry because what he really wanted was love not sex. He wanted to connect, relate, and bond, with you.

Husbands and wives should make every effort for their lovemaking to be the best that it can be. The only way that is going to happen is for both of you to take pride in what you are offering you mate. With a little creativity as well as forethought,

> Your love life does not have to be boring or predictable.

things between the two of you can sizzle, but it requires effort from both of you.

Your bedroom is your pleasure zone where your desires are satisfied as you delight and enjoy the presence of your lover. This should be the place where you can truly relax, receive love, and be cared for. Never complain about what you allow. Either remain silent or get the courage to do something about it. In your private love chamber, a man and a woman should be able to experience tranquility and all the joys associated with being married.

## The Frustrated Man

There is a difference between a sexy woman and a woman who has sex. A sexy woman is in tune with her sexuality and the expressions of such. She has an appetite for sexual pleasure and enjoys being the object of affection and desire. She is uninhibited by life's non-sexual challenges. Sexual intimacy is at the forefront of her mind. Her sexuality is the embodiment of who she is; she owns it and wears it like a sweet-smelling fragrance. Due to her own desires, sexual gratification is a priority in her life.

On the other hand, the woman who has sex out of duty, obligation, or solely for personal needs stifles bilateral desire. Also, if sexual desire is unilateral (one-sided) the other side will walk away unfulfilled. Although, the sexual encounter between the two may be explosive, it does not erase the craving of the man to be with a sexy woman.

When sex is preformed out of duty, in both the male and the female, desire is DWARFED and overshadowed by the chore of (duty). Inside every woman, there's a reservoir of sex appeal. A sexy woman is one who is constantly making withdrawals from that within. The woman who has sex is sexy, however, her sex appeal is in a state of dormancy.

The woman, who has sex out of duty or obligation, wants to be viewed in the eyes of her husband as a sexy woman. But in all honesty, she is not, and if he verbalizes his feelings than he is attacked, condemned, and falsely accused. But wait, hold up, slow your role, it's time to face the music - you are asking him to celebrate who you are not. That, in and of itself, is wrong.

Your self-imposed image is clashing with your reality. The image that you have of yourself is not matching the woman you are displaying. Either change the image or fix the reality. I am so desperately trying to help you, the missing component here is desire. In the wholesome confines of marriage desire is the fuel of sex. Outside of marriage it is fueled by lust.

Sex out of obligation is like a two-edge sword: on one hand, it relieves sexual tension, but on the other hand it blocks emotional intimacy. Once again, either change the image or fix the reality because you can't have it both ways. Being the object of another's desire is not just something women crave, but it is something men crave as well. Lack of desire on either part (personal & for him) stirs sexual frustration.

## Key Points

- Sex is not the creation of man, it is God's gift to man.

- A healthy sex life should be a major priority for each couple.

- The husband and wife are equally responsible for their romantic atmosphere.

- Failure to meet each other's proper sexual needs is a violation of your marital duties.

- Couples should strive for intimacy in every area of their life.

- When your spouse's sexual flames erupt, it is your emergency and obligation to extinguish their flames of passion.

- Energy is required for lovemaking. A lazy lover is not a wise lover.

# The Journey Continues...

# FIVE

## The Power Of Femininity

Adam was the first victim of this mysterious phenomenon labeled "the bite of pleasure," but in no way was he the last one to succumb to its powerful effects. Wealth nor strength exempts one from the bite of pleasure.

In the mid-seventies as a little boy in church, I use to hear the preacher tell the following story from time to time. A woman got on a crowded bus with people standing in the aisles. One man who was standing said to another man who was sitting, "Be a gentleman, give the woman your seat." The sitting man looked up at the woman then looked back at the man and said, "she's dressed like a man, smoking like a man, looking like a man, let her stand up like a man." This story always produced a chuckle in the church. What was the sitting man really saying? I will explore this over the next several pages. It's apparent that the sitting gentleman was disturbed by the feminist movement of the 1960s and did not embrace the advances of women.

One of the hardest things for people to do is change. There's an instinctive resistance against altering one's belief or long held opinions. The feminist movement fought for change. The belief was that a woman should be permitted to have economic, political, and social equality with man. Those long held traditional views regarding women as inferior, and less important than men were indeed wrong. To many women of that day, their acts were justifiable. The feminist movement first fought for legal equality, especially the right to vote. The movement later focused attention on job discrimination. Most professional careers such as law, politics, and medicine were closed to women. The movement faced strong opposition because many believed the woman's place was in the home caring for the children, cleaning, and preparing meals. But was the 1800s and 1900s the start of the feminist movement? No, it wasn't. The movement started in antiquity, as written in the Bible, in (I Corinthians 11:3-16).

The women of Corinthians demanded the same treatment as men - similar to many women today. They regarded marriage and raising children as unjust restrictions of their rights. The women of Corinthians lived in a male dominated culture where most women were treated as nothing more than humble servants. Asserting their independence, the women began demanding jobs traditionally held by men. The women abandoned all signs of femininity when they started wearing men's clothing, hairstyles and conducting themselves as men. Husbands often traded or even disposed of their wives at will. Most wives were one mishap away from receiving a hand-written bill of divorce. As you can see, the advances of women have come a long way, but at what price?

During the process to gain economic, political, and social equality, womanliness has been sacrificed. A large segment of our society is so busy competing against the traditional views of the male role and the female role until femininity has gotten lost in the equation. Top this off with the loss of etiquette, manners, sophistication, elegance, and civility. You now have a glimpse of how a large segment of men observes the opposite sex. In this modern day of women's lib, I am convinced the feminist movement helped and hurt the cause of women. Not to offend anyone, I do believe in equal pay and equal rights, yet the notion that a woman can do anything a man can do is ludicrous. All of us need to accept and realize the male and female are different by design.

Some women have failed to recognize that the feminine quality is what attracts, stimulates, inspires, as well as motivates men. The feminist movement has reduced women's femininity. For some women, being feminine is almost something to be ashamed of. Feminine women can be viewed as weak, soft, delicate, fragile, vulnerable, and inadequate. As a result, some women feel they must:

- Dress and talk like a man.

- Demand power and control like a man.

- Compete like a man.

- Dip, spit, chew, and smoke like a man.

- Be tough like a man by playing football, boxing, weightlifting, wrestling, and racing cars.

I am not speaking for all men; some men don't have a problem with any of the above. They are certainly entitled to their individual perspective, but for the average fellow, these same things are a turn off not a turn on. Men are not attracted to those manly traits that some women portray. To avoid criticism or being labeled, a large segment of men has silenced themselves concerning feminism. Am I saying that women who engage in all the above are not feminine? I can't make that assumption based on a single act or undertaking. I am simply pointing out that no one should cease to be who the Creator designed them to be just to gain a status with another.

Ladies, you can't have it both ways. On one hand you are saying respect and treat me like a woman, but on the other hand, you treat and conduct yourself like a man. Just because you are bold enough to say a thing, doesn't make it right. Also, just because you can do a thing, doesn't mean you should.

Medical technology will allow a man to have a sex change, but I don't see long lines awaiting the procedure. Rights should not be confused with the purpose of why we are placed here. Civil disobedience is one thing, but the erosion of the unique quality that united the first man and woman "femininity" should not be lost or sacrificed to be equal with man.

In the Garden of Eden, you can say Adam fell in love with femininity. The woman was feminine; therefore, you could say Adam gave femininity the name, Eve. One of the first things the mother of all living humans possessed was femininity. She was all woman! God then presents the feminine woman to the masculine man.

There is a natural power or influence that women possess over man. This power exists because the "rib" was taken out of the man to create woman. Within the male, there is an indescribable desire to be reconnected with what God removed from him and placed within the woman. Women have a natural power to influence a man without using force. This natural power of influence

> Femininity
> means
> "Womanliness"

is pulling the man toward her and toward her desires. It is an inherent lure. The power of femininity can be used in a positive or negative manner - for good or for evil. This chapter is *not* about women using femininity to seduce men for personal gain.

When God formed man, man did not become a living soul until God breathed the breath of life into his nostril (Gen 2:7). God placed His *spirit* into man, then he placed the *God-spirit rib* of man into woman, and God arranged for the male child and female child to come from the woman. All humans *share the womb connection* and all wombs share the *rib connection* and the *rib of the woman plus the man encases the God connection.*

Most of the world believes in a higher power. Why? It is because humans are walking around with a part of God on the inside of them and what was placed on the inside craves a connection with that source. This hunger or thirst will not be satisfied until the soul or spirit of man touches the source of life. This is why when a man or woman makes a connection through salvation, things appear to be new. They've found new joy, peace, and happiness and life takes on a brand-new meaning. So, it is with the male and the female.

When the craving for what's missing within touches or connects with femininity, this intangible, invisible attraction will pull a man to a woman to meet her needs and desires. It doesn't matter if we are talking about changing a tire for a female stranger or giving up his coat to a woman when it's cold outside. Femininity is powerful and is not an attribute you can turn on or off. Please don't confuse what I'm referencing with sexual attraction, but if you add *physical attraction* with the *desire to meet her needs* you will have an explosion of two powerful forces.

A woman can accomplish more as a woman than she can conducting herself as a man. In the confines of marriage when a wife fights for mutual fairness and refuses to be submissive to her husband's position as leader, she must be very careful not to send the message that she is fighting to be equal with her husband. The reason why this is so very important is that real men are not gentle with other men. We don't treat other men delicate or soft and we're definitely not sensitive to them. To be direct with you, men actually resent a man who is overly sensitive. Ladies, embrace your femininity.

Once a man regards a woman as an equal,
he will treat her as an equal.

Men do not necessarily need to be held when emotionally upset. If he views you as an equal, he may reject or be hesitant to hold you when you're upset. In his mind, subconsciously he feels that you are alright because he would be alright. Most men do not need romance per se. Sex will do just fine, thank you very much. If he looked upon you as an equal, he may stop attempting to be romantic as well. Women must take a fundamental look at the things they fight and debate over.

The military is a primary example. I do not believe a woman should be placed in a combat role, but I would like to point out a disparity here. A woman will join the army like a man, want the pay and respect of a man, but not be allowed to fight or possibly die like a man. Don't misunderstand me. Despite their supportive status, female soldiers are indeed dying. However, in every war, male soldiers are dying by the thousands while for the most part, female soldiers are returning home. Where is the equality here? Please remember when you are barking like a man, dressing, acting, talking, and displaying anger like a man, it's possible that someone may treat you like a man.

## Femininity Effects On Men

A woman danced at a king's birthday party. The dance pleased him, and he swore to give her whatever she wanted up to half of his kingdom. Her request was the head of the preacher. Because of the power of femininity, a man was beheaded all because another man lost his mind over a woman.

Matthew 14: 6-11

*"When Herod's birthday was kept, the daughter of Herodias danced before them and pleased Herod. Whereupon he promised with an oath to give her whatsoever she would ask. And she, being before instructed of her mother, said give me here John Baptist's head in a charger. And the king was sorry: nevertheless for the*

*oath's sake and them which sat with him at meat, he commanded it to be given her. And he sent, and beheaded John in the prison. And his head was brought in a charger, and given to the damsel: and she brought it to her mother."*

Notice "she pleased the king" not through serving him, nor in a sexual manner. Remember when a man touches or connects with femininity, it produces a natural desire within the male to satisfy the needs and wishes of the woman. There are at least four reasons why John the Baptist lost his head:

1. King was pleased by a dance.

2. King had an oath.

3. King was sitting in the presence of men.

4. King hated John the Baptist.

## Samson and Delilah

When you think of Samson, you may think to yourself how foolish can one man be? It's easy to feel that way when you're not emotionally attached to a situation. We all have seen a woman being abused by a man who says he loves her. As bystanders, we comment with confidence that we would exit the relationship. The truth of the matter is, if you were facing the same set of circumstances, you may find yourself doing the same thing. Like her, you would struggle with your emotions. Your head will be leading you one way while your heart is leading you another, and getting out of the relationship becomes more difficult for the individual in question. When the head and the heart are together, deciding is simple, but how can one arrive at a decision when the head and the heart are not together? It's crucial that each of us understand some decisions you'll make with your head and some decisions you will make with your heart.

Samson would have saved himself a whole lot of trouble if he had made his decision with his head. As you will clearly see, his emotion led him amiss. Samson knew Delilah could not be trusted. He knew she was plotting and scheming, yet he told her the source of his power. Why? Four reasons:

1. Samson was in love.

Judges 16:4

"It came to pass afterward that he loved a woman in the Valley of Sorek, whose name was Delilah."

2. Samson was lured in by the power of femininity "womanliness"

Judges 16:5

...and the lords of the Philistines came up to her and said to her, entice him and see wherein his great strength lieth.

3. Samson wanted to please Delilah.

Judges 16:15

"And she said unto him, how canst thou say, I love thee, when thine heart is not with me? Thou hast mocked me these three times, and hast not told me wherein thy great strength lieth."

4. Samson got tired of her daily nagging. She vexed his soul.

Judges 16:16-17

"And it came to pass when she pressed him daily with her words and urged him so, that his soul was vexed unto death, that he told her all his heart."

Therefore, if you mix love and the power of femininity with a righteous or lustful desire to please along with daily seductions, an explosion takes place in the soul of man. Delilah became a challenge for Samson. In his mind, it was an intriguing, exciting and a stimulating game to extract from him the source of his strength. Whether it was true or not, she convinced Samson with her daily enticement and charm that she loved him. She made him feel important, powerful, and strong and he was considering his many prevailing exploits. Of course, Samson made other mistakes, those are for another time.

As a result of being controlled and enticed, one becomes subject to the desires of him or her. When a relationship has been saturated with an enormous amount of desire, to satisfy or not to satisfy, one will struggle to maintain their uprightness. The bite of pleasure is simply the after effects of being satisfied or charmed by a woman or a man. The after affects can be good or bad. In this period of time the chemistry and bond, between one or both, appear to be unbreakable.

Samson, like so many men today, got caught up in the trap of thinking he could handle the enticement; he deceived himself. Well, he could *not* handle it! In a situation like this, once your emotions become charged, a burning desire to satisfy and to be satisfied overwhelms the victim. Never confuse the bite of pleasure with the bait of pleasure. The aim of one is to please or to satisfy another (Adam), while the aim of the other is to deceive or to destroy another (Samson).

## BACK TO THE GARDEN OF EDEN

Genesis 2:21-22

*"And the Lord God caused a deep sleep to fall upon Adam, and he slept: and he took one of his ribs, and closed up the flesh instead thereof. And the rib, which the Lord God had taken from man made he a woman, and brought her unto the man."*

God takes a rib from the man to create woman so when womanliness touches manliness here is what you have. There's a connection, closeness, bond, a grip on the individual seat of emotion, the "soul." This grip compels you to satisfy, at all costs, the desires of the object of your affection.

If you are talking about position or wealth, the woman may very well be powerless; however, right or wrong, if her womanliness touches his manliness, she's more powerful than the most powerful male. God himself took from Adam to give to Eve. Eve has a way of taking from Adam to give to Eve.

> How can a powerless woman bring down a powerful man? President Bill Clinton and Monica Lewinskie

The effects on the one under the influence can be described in a number of ways. The experience of the male and the female are similar, yet different. What they are feeling can be depicted as love, lust, infatuation, and overcharged emotions stimulated by a strong sexual lure. Accept it or reject it, there's a transfer of spirits here. The influenced individual is not his or her self and will do things totally out of character. Yes, they did it, but that's not who they are. They are truly living under the influence of another.

You have heard of driving under the influence.
Well, he is living under the influence.

The man was the first gift the woman consciously acknowledged, but man was not the first gift the woman received. Woman's first gift came from the Creator. It was the gift of femininity and how He uniquely and marvelously made her. Every woman should strive to possess and maintain the creation of woman's originality. With open arms men all over the world will gladly receive the feminine daughters of Eve.

## Key Points

- The uniqueness and inborn lure of the woman are undeniable.

- Woman's first gift came from the Creator. It was the gift of femininity and how He marvelously made her.

- Maintaining feminine qualities does not make a woman weak or inferior to man.

- Male and female are truly designed differently, and the difference should be celebrated not hated.

- The bite of pleasure is simply the after effects of being satisfied or charmed by a woman or a man.

- The power of femininity can be used for good or for bad.

- When a man touches or connects with femininity, it produces a natural desire within the male to satisfy the needs and wishes of the woman.

# The Journey Continues...

# Six

## Maintaining The Marital Bond

> Humanity's first couple, Adam and Eve, were not exempt from the predator of their day. Although non-human, a predator nonetheless. In some form or fashion every relationship under the heavens will be confronted by a predator (outside love interest). Like Adam and Eve, the predator is after your bond.

If your marriage is wonderful and your mate is everything you can ask for, you are certainly one of the blessed ones. I applaud and celebrate you. Never ever lose what you have. Love is great when it's functioning properly. When both parties are totally saturated and content within the relationship, success awaits, yet by no means should a couple permit their guard to come down. Their relationship still needs to be fortified against the many obstacles to maintain a healthy marriage.

My focus with this chapter is the *other* woman/man. To keep things simple, let me just say it - ADULTERY. There was a time when the wedding ring meant something to the one wearing the ring as well as the onlooker eye balling the ring. My, how things have changed! Each generation is becoming bolder than the previous one. Before attempting to catch the eye of your spouse, the other man or woman used to wait until they were outside of your presence. Nowadays, they are squeezing and teasing, winking, and blinking, certainly not thinking, right in front of you.

We live in a predatory society. Seducing spirits are all around us. In the doctor's office, department and convenient stores, restaurants, workplace, gymnasium, church, home and even your circle of friends. We must safeguard our marriages against any seductive brother or sister. I am not condoning any act of unfaithfulness or making excuses for a wayward heart in marriage. Both emotional and physical affairs are wrong. With the following statements, I simply want to point out the difference between the predator spouse, victim spouse, and knowledgeable spouse.

The predator spouse is looking for an opportunity to be unfaithful. They are the hunter. The one with the plan, scheme, and the pick-up line. If he or she spots a potential prey who is willing, married or single, short or tall, pretty or not, he or she will attempt to capture their victim.

The victim spouse is naïve, innocent, unsuspecting, immature, or green. He or she got caught up in a compromising situation. Unaware, the signs were there - roadblock, detour, bridge is out, curve ahead, speeding fines doubled, yield, no passing, stop, etc. The victim spouse simply misread the signs and when signs are misread an accident is waiting to happen and very well may happen. In either case, the pain is the same for the predator and the victim significant other.

The knowledgeable spouse is aware of the flirtatious nature of a married or single individual. He/she is excited, stimulated, enjoys, and even appreciates the attention shown. The spouse who engages in such dangerous behavior may flirt themselves and may even be willing to follow this road until the end. The knowledgeable spouse can, at will, convert to a predatory spouse, but for the most part they are primarily a responder. They will not initiate the encounter; however, if you let them know you are willing to play house they are willing to play also.

The sequence looks like this:

- Predator spouse pursues the victim spouse or available individual

- Predator spouse pursues the knowledgeable spouse or available individual

- Knowledgeable spouse converts and pursues the victim spouse or available individual

- Knowledgeable spouse makes themselves available to the married or single predator.

It appears some couples are closer in the beginning of their relationship than they are in the middle or the end. The longer you are with your spouse the more connected your lives should be. The bond should grow stronger not weaker! I have no facts or data to support the following comments, but it is being reported that women are having affairs more often than their male counterparts.

Women often make the comment, "All men are dogs." All men are *not* dogs. My question to women who make this comment is, "Who are men cheating with?" They are cheating and having affairs with…women. I hear you, I hear you, but that subject matter (bisexual men) is for another day and another time.

I am noticing a trend. Women are more worried about another woman chasing their husband instead of their husband chasing another woman. It's a woman attempting to seduce your man. It's a woman attempting him to leave you for her.

Marriage is a wonderful institution, and no one should come between the sacredness of this union. The challenge for couples to maintain the purity of their relationship is greater now than it has ever been. A man or woman can get sex when he or she cannot get food to eat. For too many people, sex is just something you do to feel good; no love or commitment is involved whatsoever. If you're married, through your everyday actions, you should send a message to all potential spouse seekers - the position is already filled!

- Any openings soon? No

- Are you accepting applications? No

- Are you hiring in the future? No

When you master the art of pleasing your spouse, you will be able to respond in the above manner. Now, let's learn more about what to do and what not to do. The shortest distance between two points is a straight line. Envision a rope or a cord if you will. A leveled rope or cord eliminates slackness. Where love is concerned, the leveled rope or cord represents stability, soundness, or the unsinkability of love. If the husband and wife are connected at the heart (in tuned with each other and balanced) and if their bond is strong, there's no space or opportunity for another to come between the two of them. In a case like this, the needs of both spouses are being met and the relationship is healthy.

Slackness (inconsistency) creates opportunity

Now if the husband or wife is on an emotional roller coaster in between their peaks and valleys, this is where the other man or woman is allowed entry into your relationship. Depending upon the offense, this is the place where you or your spouse may struggle with faithfulness. This is the place of susceptibility. At this point, the husband and wife have made it convenient for another person to penetrate their relationship. It may never happen, and your partner may not even give it a second thought, but on the other hand, you may be thinking they're totally committed to you and committed to the church. Besides this, I am sure you can think of a whole list of things wrong with him or her.

You're right, it may never happen, but don't be the one to place your relationship in a situation for it to happen. Seek to be all that you can be in the relationship. If your spouse violates the marriage covenant you can walk away, if you so desire, knowing that the demise was not caused by you. If a couple lives in a constant state of frustration, anger, bitterness, resentfulness, animosity, and hostility, their bond or closeness is weakening due to constant strain. Straining stretches you and it also hurts.

When it comes to your significant other the position of straining is not where you want them to be.

Since the husband and wife are no longer meeting the emotional needs of each other, here is where the danger lies. The couple is now conducting themselves like lost tourists in a strange town with criminal activity all around. Here they are driving a Rolls Royce with a personalized license plate, wearing expensive clothing, diamonds, and money hanging outside of the purse. Would you agree these tourists are simply asking to be robbed? Their actions are saying, "Please! Mr. Robber. Here I am, rob me!"

Do all tourists get robbed because of bad judgment or for making a mistake? Of course not. In your relationship, this is not where you want to be because you may very well get robbed. Consequently, every relationship in a precarious situation will not lead to an affair or divorce nor should it. Please keep in mind, if you are not meeting the needs of your spouse, you are giving another male or female the opening to do so. One of the reasons we don't reach resolution is because we've stopped competing. Never forget for a moment you are still competing. Sound ridiculous? Keep reading!

Within the same week a wife could hear the following comments from her husband and a coworker.

Husband:

- His morning greeting, "Yaw!"
- Not now! The game is on.
- All you do is nag.
- Why didn't you pay the bills like I told you to?
- You are gaining too much weight.
- I am too busy to do lunch.
- That's a bad idea.
- Flowers are a waste of money.
- Do it yourself.
- You're always late. You have no respect for time.

Coworker:

- Good morning, Susan.
- I have time to listen.
- What's wrong? Talk to me.
- You are so orderly and efficient.
- You look great!
- Can I buy you lunch?
- That's a good idea.
- Here, I brought you a little friendly something.
- Let me help you with that.
- I love your promptness.

Whose words made her feel good about herself? The husband?
Wrong!

Who built her self- esteem up? Coworker? Right!

Who was kind, considerate, and thoughtful? Husband? Wrong!

Who made her feel valued? Coworker? Right!

Let's look at what has happened. The husband has become Mr.
Wrong and the coworker has become Mr. Right. So, the wife may

find herself thinking about Mr. Right more and Mr. Wrong less. This same state of affairs can be reversed. I am only reminding you that the same thing it took to get your spouse is needed to keep them. There's an old proverb that says one man's trash is another's treasure. Never take for granted that someone will love to have what you are taking for granted. Simply put, someone would love to take your place.

Maintaining one's bond will not only benefit the husband and wife, but the children and society profit as well. If our homes are destroyed, every other entity of society is affected in some way. The family unit is the foundation which everything else hinges.

After several years of marriage, one of the biggest problems couples face is in the area of communication. Because of poor communication, the understanding between the husband and wife begins to suffer. The Holy Scripture admonishes us "out of all your getting get an understanding."

Over the years, I've come to understand that a lack of understanding will lead to a misunderstanding. Relationships suffer when the husband and wife no longer understand each other. You can't drive a car or program a computer without having an understanding. The purpose of higher education is to provide understanding to the masses. If a university fails to educate its students, it will not be in operation very long. The same is true concerning a healthy marriage. If a couple fails to understand the heart and inherent makeup of each other, the continuity of the relationship will be lost. Thinking you understand your spouse is not necessarily understanding them. When we get married! We must remember that we are not marrying a finished product. I am not today what I was yesterday, and I will not be tomorrow what I am today.

Mentally, we are still developing and every day our thinking should be challenged to expand. Each mate should be seeking to embrace and understand the person their spouse is blossoming into. If each person's growth and development are for the good of the relationship, this growth should be welcome. Your marriage should be fresh and alive. Each day we should learn something new.

In the case of adultery, what if the lesson learned by you or your spouse resulted in pain? What should you do? Experience is not the best teacher, nevertheless it is one of the teachers of life. Your relationship may take a serious blow. The damage caused may appear to be fatal or non-repairable. If your marriage survives the attack, the attack cannot become the center of your focus. Your focus must be understanding *why* the attack took place and strengthening your relationship against further attacks. All else will only contribute to the further demise of the relationship.

What happens when we fail to embrace the growth of our mate? The couple turns into what I call the teacher/student relationship. At any given time, the husband or the wife may find themselves repeatedly instructing or attempting to enlighten their spouse. One has become the teacher and their spouse the student. They will teach lesson after lesson and give example after example hoping their spouse will grasp the wisdom offered, but to no avail. The student who is not receiving what the teacher is presenting then converts to the teacher role because he or she feels the other one doesn't fully understand what they're attempting to convey. This scenario will repeat itself repeatedly with neither party accomplishing their desired goal. The problem with this is neither of them is hearing the other. Both are simply informing the other one of some fact or point to support how they feel.

Men communicate from the aspect of facts. Give us the facts to support what you are conversing. Women communicate mainly from an emotional aspect. The dilemma worsens because the man is screaming out particulars; while the woman is voicing her feelings. She's thinking he really doesn't get it. Because of the teacher/ student role, the husband and wife become more and more frustrated living with each other as well as communicating with each other.

I have learned a valuable lesson in life concerning disputes. *It's not always who's right, but what's right.* Stop thinking you're right all the time! If you're always right, this means your spouse is always wrong. News Flash! Everyone is capable of error. Depending on the subject matter, both of you could be wrong. You see, amid your hostile environment, if what's right has gotten lost, it *is* possible that the presented explanations, augments, or facts are irrelevant to the real issue.

Good communication skills, requires listening as well as speaking. It also requires processing and understanding what one has heard. When couples fail to do this, they will suffer from what I call communication congestion. To help you fully understand this terminology, think about congestion on a freeway. Congestion on a freeway occurs when something or somebody ahead interrupts the flow of motorists, such as an accident, construction, or simply too many vehicles on the road at the same time. When this congestion occurs, it becomes difficult to reach one's destination on time. Now, keep in mind we are not speaking of one motorist being delayed, but hundreds or possibly thousands.

## Communication Congestion

Like congestion on a freeway, communication congestion is hundreds or thousands of conversations that did not reach their destination. It is unfinished discussions that did not reach the heart or penetrate the walls of your mate's understanding. There are times no matter how you express yourself, for whatever reason, your mate fails to receive the desired message, so out of anger, frustration, or the mere unwillingness to fight, you abandon the conversation.

Over time, the abandoned or dropped conversations become congested with other abandoned or dropped conversations. You end up with several years of marriage and thousands of unfinished, unresolved issues that failed to reach or accomplish their intended purpose.

## Conflicts In Marriage

The number one issue in marriage is the inability to resolve conflicts. The bible gives us six rules to resolve conflicts.

1. Have a mind to please each other

2. Practice humility

3. Seek to understand

4. Be a peacemaker

5. Practice forgiveness

6. Show compassion for the other

Romans 12: 16-21

*"Be of the same mind one toward another. Mind not high things, but condescend to men of low estate. Be not wise in your own conceits. Recompense to no man evil for evil. Provide things honest in the sight of all men. If it be possible, as much as lieth in you, live peaceably with all men. Dearly beloved, avenge not yourselves, but rather give place unto wrath: for it is written vengeance is mines; I will repay, saith the Lord. Therefore if thy enemy hunger feed him; if he thrist give him drink: for in So doing thou shalt heap coals of fire on his head. Be not overcome of evil, but overcome evil with good."*

## Friendship

Friendship is the *sun* of marriage. What the sun is to Earth, friendship is to marriage. Remaining friends is the pathway to maintaining your marital bond. Friendless marriages sometimes produce sexless marriages which by the way lead to divorce. A new house and a new automobile have something in common, both require maintenance. Maybe not at first, but if you want the home to continue to look good or the automobile to keep running well, maintenance will be required. This maintenance mindset should be noted and maintained in marriage. Friendship produces emotional closeness and emotional closeness leads to a deeper level of intimacy. Like a key unlocking a lock, maintaining the friendship unlocks the heart, soul, and sexual expression of your significant other.

## Marriage Delivers Us From Selfishness

Adam, the first man who was truly living the single life had to be delivered from selfishness. Before Eve was created it was all about Adam and what Adam wanted to do. After the fall of man, his selfish ways returned.

Gen 3:12

*"And the man said, the woman whom thou gavest to be with me, she gave me of the tree and I did eat."*

Allow me to translate Adam's words. Read what Adam *really* said to God:

- God, there were no problems between us until you gave me the woman.
- I was doing fine all by myself until you gave me the woman.
- I didn't disobey your command until you gave me the woman.
- Hey! Share in the blame. You gave me the woman.

Adam blames God and the woman for his predicament, but remember marriage and the woman came to deliver him from selfishness. The root of all conflicts revolves around one word - selfishness. You can have it your way at the burger place, but selfishness will not produce a healthy marriage. It can't all be your way or their way.

## Mothered or Smothered

Have you noticed that there is only one letter separating the word mothering from smothering? Wives need to be very careful in their attempt to create a loving, caring environment, so they don't smother the flames of their relationship. A little mothering is healthy. Men will enjoy and appreciate the extra care and concern, but too much becomes troublesome as well as burdensome. His passion or hobbies may not be your passion or hobbies. When a wife demands a say so in every aspect of a man's life, it is only a matter of time before her consistent, intrusive, involvement becomes a detriment of her and the man she supposedly loves.

Most people can deal with crowds, but not being crowded. One can be a part of a crowd and yet maintain a certain amount of space within the crowd. Well, relationships are no different. The family unit, obligations, responsibility, and duties make up the crowd, but amid the crowd the husband and the wife still need their space. Therefore, both the husband and wife need to be careful not to smother one another. Remember, there's only one letter separating mothering from smothering and both the husband and the wife will resist being smothered.

## The Emotional Doctor

You are the emotional doctor for your relationship. Every doctor uses his/her ears, eyes, and hands to treat a patient. The same is true for married couples. You must use your ears, eyes, and hands in your relationship.

**Eyes:** Couples must recognize the strength and problem areas of their relationship. Sometimes we are up too close or too closed to see what we're really doing to each other. Words have power and will affect your mate in a positive or negative manner. You must see the hurt and pain you are causing them and like any good medical doctor, give the patient your best possible care.

**Ears:** You must hear the heart of your mate and take it to heart. You must listen not to disagree, but to strengthen the communication between the two of you. You must hear what is being said without interpreting what is said. If every time a couple engages in meaningful conversation and all they discuss is their differences, communication will be strained or stifled. There's a different point of view on everything conceivable. Communication must flow like a river or it will be reduced to a stream.

**Hands:** Your relationship is in your hands. You can't blame others for what you have failed to treat properly. Like a dentist, all treatments are not the same. There are times when cleanings, fillings, replacements, or extractions are required. There are some things in your marriage that need to be cleaned up - your attitude, the way you communicate, your home, the way you express love, or your mind. Some cavities need to be filled with honesty and forgiveness. Also, there are some things that need to be extracted. Identify these areas and have the courage to apply the proper treatment for a healthy relationship.

Problem areas must be resolved. Seek the advice of a knowledgeable counselor, pastor, or friend who can assist in ending your war. You know, there's a difference between a fight and a war. Maintain your bond because it's better to keep what one has than to regain what one had.

## Key Points

- Adultery is a serious threat to all marriages.
- Never forget you are still competing.
- Slackness creates opportunity.
- Mr. Right is looking for Mrs. Right and she is looking for him.
- Take ownership of your relationship.
- Get an understanding if you don't get anything else.
- Selfishness produces conflicts.
- Good communication skills are a necessary tool for combating conflict.

# The Journey Continues...

# Seven

## VITAL INFORMATION

> Before the fall, God gave humanity's first couple,
> Adam and Eve, information to survive. He gave
> them *vital* information.

Gen 2:16-17

*"Of every tree of the garden thou mayest freely eat, but of the tree of the knowledge of good and evil, thou shalt not eat of it: for in the day that thou eatest thereof thou shalt surely die."*

In the courting days, we do everything possible to satisfy our mate. We are at our best. We act and conduct ourselves as a genie and the wish of our love's interest, our master, is our command. Fresh young love. Wow!

Why can't we remain in this zone forever? Is it possible? We love the feeling, we're excited, and it shows. In the beginning stages of love, everything is new. Newness creates excitement, and everything is automatic. You dress, talk, feel, and think the part. You want him or her to like you as much as you like them. With both parties enthused to meet the emotional needs of the other, everything is just wonderful. After a few years of courting or marriage, the things that came automatically become work, and who wants to work at love?

> Vital information must be adhered to and not ignored. Adam and Eve's story is all too familiar.

Love is easy. Love is easier for some than for others, but love is work - inside and outside of the home. It's also work to love your enemies, people who hate you without a cause, and people who have betrayed your trust and repeatedly disappointed or hurt you. It's work because it's unnatural for a man or woman to pursue pain. The mind has a way of reminding us of our painful experiences.

## Dual Love Transmission

Man's ingenuity has given the world many wonderful devices to make life easier. We have clocks, telephones, computers, and automobiles to name a few. An automobile is a marvelous machine, and with all it's capable of doing, driving is extremely pleasurable.

The transmission is the part of an automobile that carries over power from the engine to the rear axle. It's the set of gears that determines the relative speed. The two types of transmissions are an automatic and a standard shift.

**Automatic:** No work required! You select the drive and the transmission will shift without human intervention.

**Standard:** Work is required! The driver must engage the clutch and shift each gear manually.

In the beginning stages of learning to drive a standard shift, nearly everyone will experience some herky-jerky motion. This motion shows and tells everyone watching that an inexperienced driver is behind the wheel. The challenge, at first, is knowing when to shift gears. If you shift too early you will discover the difficulty getting the gears to engage, plus the vehicle will somewhat stall. If you shift too late, the engine will race strenuously. It would have been so much easier if all we had to do was count one, two, three, shift. One, two, three, shift. Unfortunately, that's not the way it is.

The speed of the engine determines when the driver should shift gears and what gear the driver should be in.

Am I telling you that you'll need to watch the speedometer, the road, and maybe even the gear stick while engaging the clutch with your left foot and easing off the gas with your right foot as your right hand changes the gear? Yes, with a few exceptions, you should only glance at the speedometer and the gear stick. I am so grateful I did not see the written instructions prior to learning to drive a standard shift. The instructions alone have the capability to frighten all new drivers. The more you drive a standard shift the better you'll become. You'll gradually discover you're becoming less dependent on your eyes and more dependent on other faculties.

The driver now relies on:

**Ears:** Listening to the sound of the engine and making the determination to shift before the engine begins to strain.

**Feel:** The driver no longer needs to glance at the gear stick, yet has developed a feel for the gears.

Most individuals prefer an automatic transmission over a standard primarily because less work is involved. You simply place it in gear and go. I have seen automobiles with dual gas tanks and steering wheels. Conceive if you will that man has created a vehicle with dual transmissions and every vehicle manufactured is equipped with an automatic and a standard shift transmission. One car, two transmissions. Like the conceivable concept of one car having two transmissions, married couples go through what I like to refer to as the dual transmissions of love. To a couple's lack of knowledge, their relationship has been equipped with both transmissions - the automatic and the standard shift. Somehow our mindset has been conditioned to consider the automatic gear only.

*For simplicity, allow me to interchange the word gear with the word mode.*

We get married and drive along for a few years in the automatic mode, then at some point, without any warning, everything switches. The relationship shifts from the automatic mode to the standard mode and now work is required to give your mate what you once so freely gave. It now takes a little effort to dress, talk, feel, and think the part.

We get lazy and don't want to work at love. While in the standard shift mode, we fail to shift. The reason we're not shifting is because we don't realize shifting is required; therefore, the relationship begins to strain. In the beginning stages of learning to drive a standard shift, some gears are easier to shift than others. Whether you remember it or not, you probably struggled with a gear.

There may be areas in your relationship where some things still appear to be automatic. This may be true, yet it's very important to understand the mechanism of the dual process. It is switching back and forth between the automatic mode and the standard mode which is why you are totally satisfied with one area of your relationship and perhaps somewhat dissatisfied with another.

In the automatic mode, our mate will freely supply our needs and are willing to satisfy our heart's desires. In the standard mode, work is required to satisfy our heart's desires. Every couple will experience this to some degree. Your relationship is perfectly normal. The challenge is to learn how to shift smoothly without the herky-jerky motion associated with learning to drive a standard shift.

## The Relationship Standard Modes

**First Gear:** *Smooth* - There is a bump here and there. You are still learning one another's likes and dislikes. Marriage is great, and you are extremely happy.

**Second Gear:** *Working on it* - Problems are beginning to mount. Things are not perfect, yet the good days still outweigh the bad days. Patience, forgiveness, and understanding help you through it. Your love and commitment remain strong.

**Third Gear:** *Disagreements* - Things are difficult between the two of you. You're facing hard times with more bad days than good days. Couples finding themselves in the third gear must discover a way to shift down, not up. Every effort must be made to prevent your relationship from going to the next mode.

**Fourth Gear:** *Contemplating divorce* - You're convinced the two of you will be better off without each other. This whole thing has been one big mistake - so you think.

The difference between a love transmission and a manual transmission is love transmission doesn't have to go through all the gears. You simply find the gear that's working for you and stay there. With the manual transmission, your rate of speed must determine the proper gear. If a couple ever finds themselves in the fourth gear or "mode" this is not the place you want to be. The fourth gear is the breaking point in the relationship, but even here the relationship can be saved.

Forgiveness, patience, healing, and understanding, if applied, will help overcome all the hurt and pain. The harmony in the relationship can be restored, but it requires much work. Still, if the relationship continues to move forward at a high rate of speed, it may very well come to an end. The surprising thing is, one is still in love with the institution of marriage. If the couple divorces, it is not marriage they are divorcing, it is the person within the marriage they are hoping to get away from. Over half of the people married are on their second or third relationship.

**Fifth Gear:** *Filing for a divorce* - It's the nail in the coffin, the ashes to ashes, and the dust to dust. One or both of you have finally made the decision to end the marriage and move on with your life. While in this mode, couples will find themselves arguing over the simplest of things - passing the remote control, scratching each other's back, going to bed at the same time, and the list can go on and on.

Everything seems to be difficult between the two of you. Your conversations with one another aren't flowing as usual. As a matter of fact, you would prefer a trip to the dentist for a root canal rather than communicating with your spouse. Because of improper shifting of the clutch and the transmission, things begin to break down on the automobile. In a relationship, if a couple doesn't learn how to shift properly between the "modes" they will be compiling damage on top of damage causing the relationship to break down.

No man or woman is willing to stay in a fight for twenty-four hours a day, seven days a week, three-hundred and sixty-five days a year. Even a boxer can rest one minute after three minutes of fighting. Knowing when to shift gears in your relationship is key. In other words, if you are stuck in third gear, it's time to end the fighting. You must find a way to either down shift or shift up.

I am not suggesting or insinuating divorce, yet I am encouraging you to shift to the position of patience, understanding, healing, and forgiveness. It is important to know when to complain and when to stop complaining - when to hold, when to fold - when to stand your ground, and when to give ground. No one is perfect and that includes you. Shocking, I know! Take two aspirins and keep reading.

## Shifting Gears Properly

In an automobile you can't go from first to fourth, the transmission wasn't designed to operate in that manner. Shifting properly is from first to second, second to third, and so forth. In your relationship, it's inconceivable to go from asking for a divorce, name calling, physical violence and then to love making. Proper shifting is to get past the hurt and the pain. Forgiveness must be administered to all the hurting areas. Only then will couples be able to function properly.

A cold hand on a warm heart - either the hand chills the heart or the heart warms the hand. You cannot expect your mate to warm up to you when everything you have been providing has been cold or frozen. You may presently drive an automatic, but if you have ever learned how to properly drive a standard shift, that knowledge will remain with you for a lifetime. You can go years without driving a standard shift, but if the need arises the knowledge is still there. Marriage is the same way. Your relationship may be riding along in the automatic mode, which is certainly the better of the two transmissions, but acquiring and maintaining the knowledge of how to operate a standard shift may prove to be valuable in the long run.

Driving a standard shift was more difficult for some than for others. Some drivers had to pull off to the side of the road and wait for more favorable conditions. Once the conditions are more suitable, they continue their drive. Orchestrating between the gears is easier for some couples than for others. You can learn how to recognize the different shifting taking place within your relationship. You can learn how to shift from one mode to another. The driver who pulled off the side of the road basically signaled a time out. Couples can also signal for a time out – time out for prayer, counseling, or a cooling off period.

## When Will I Know It's Time To Shift?

At this point, if you need me to give you the answer, please read chapter six as well as chapter seven again. You are the emotional doctor for your relationship.

### Key Points

- With or without knowledge, your relationship is switching gears.

- Know the state of your marital union.

- Straining stretches you, but straining also hurts.

- Proper shifting creates ease. Improper shifting creates problems.

- You can overcome struggles.

- Constantly update your spousal knowledge. Who are they today?

- The dissatisfied areas of your life will always receive more attention than the satisfied areas.

---

# The Journey Continues...

---

# Eight

# A COMMITMENT TO LOVE

> Genesis 2:24 reveals Adam's commitment to love.
> Adam did not allow even GOD who was his
> spiritual/earthly father to come between his
> relationship with Eve. Like Adam, you are
> committed to what you confess.

Commitment: A pledge and a promise. There are three hundred and twenty-five million people in the United States of America. We are a nation governed by laws. Can you envision life if everyone broke the pledges or promises they entered? The very foundation this nation was founded on would disintegrate; our Judicial, Legislative, and Executive branches of government would fail. If there is no commitment there can be no trust. To take an oath of office would be a worthless waste of time. Who would show up for a swearing in if we knew the oath would not be honored or upheld.

There must be a commitment to the office as well as a commitment to upholding the integrity of the office. Without commitment not only will our branches of government fail, but all other established methods of operations will fail as well. The banking, legal, and educational systems will fail because without commitment, no one could be trusted to borrow or repay the money. I won't make this chapter unreasonably long by attempting to cover every aspect of the word commitment, although I am grateful that commitment is a part of our consciousness.

## "YOU ARE COMMITTED TO WHAT YOU CONFESS."

## "YOU ARE COMMITTED TO WHAT YOU CONFESS."

We live our daily lives based on the things we make a commitment to. The car we drive, the house we live in, our place of employment, and our financial obligations are all based on a commitment. It is the promise or the pledge that allows us the luxury to live in homes and purchase automobiles that we, undoubtedly, cannot afford. If it weren't for contracts and the believability of the promissory, our lives would not be as they are. So, as you can see, it is crucial that we honor the commitments we enter. Without it the wheels of integrity, sincerity, accord, and faith in humanity would come to a halt.

When I was a teenager, I use to see newlyweds driving with cans tied to the bumper of their vehicles with the words "just married" written across their rear window. As a young man, I use to read the words "just married" and say unconsciously "just messed up." My feelings were based on some of the things I witnessed as a child. I could not fathom anyone committing themselves to a man or woman for life. *Why do it?*

Looking back, my strongly held views were based upon the environment I was reared in. At the time, marriage certainly was not in my future. How could it be? You see, most of the relationships I knew of were not filled with happiness, love, respect, trust, or honor. As a matter of fact, I saw open adultery, mental and physical abuse, abandonment, and couples living with each other and seemingly hating one another. There were women who felt their only responsibility was to cook, clean, take care of the kids and provide sexual favors for their man. If she was doing that, she felt he should be grateful, go to work, and most of all leave her alone. You had men who wanted to be the boss, but had no idea what a leader was. I didn't notice intimacy or any type of public affection with these couples. I was shocked when certain couples were expecting a baby. WOW! *How did that happen?* The individuals appeared to not even like each other. My feelings were based on the messages these couples sent the community - messages of resentment, hatred, prolonged and uncontrollable anger.

You've heard of the runaway bride. Well, these couples wanted to be the runaway spouse. Some did manage to escape what they probably felt was a living hell. I can't fully explain it, but all the negative things I witnessed affected me in a positive way. There was something steering me away from repeating the vicious cycle of physical violence on women, drug experimentation, abandoning my future family, the gangster lifestyle, as well as being on the wrong side of the law. As a child, I felt different. Not better, just different. I wanted my life to matter and count for something.

Even today, I am extremely sensitive to things I perceive as wrong - spiritual or carnal. I truly recognize that God had another path for me to take in life. As I matured, I understood most of the couples I witnessed were bad representations of the institution of marriage. I no longer regard newlyweds as having messed up their lives. Instead, they have dressed up their lives. Indeed, two are better than one. Now, let's get to the heart of this chapter.

Can you recite the marriage vows? Stop reading for a moment and see how much of the marriage vow you can recite. Most females can remember most, if not all, of the sacred vows. The average male only remembers certain parts - mainly the death part. It's sad to say, but for many, male and female, marriage feels like a death sentence. If you are married, you stood before someone and pledged to live your life performing specific duties and fulfilling certain obligations. Let's look at a snippet of the standard wedding vows.

## Standard Wedding Vows

The conductor of service - Dearly beloved, we are gathered together here in the sight of God, and in the face of this company, to join this man and this woman in holy matrimony.

Wilt thou have this woman to be thy wedded wife, to live together after God's ordinance, in the holy estate of matrimony? Wilt thou love her, comfort her, honor, and keep her, in sickness and in health; and forsaking all others, keep thee only unto her, so long as ye both shall live? Wilt thou have this man to thy wedded husband, to live together after God's ordinance, in the holy estate of matrimony? Wilt thou obey him and serve him, love, honor, and keep him in sickness and in health; and, forsaking all others, keep thee only unto him, so long as ye both shall live?

Bring back memories? It may remind you that marriage is a celebration of the love a man and a woman share. For some of you, reading those few words of commitment may have been painful. Let's look at the seriousness of the vows we exchanged.

## Making Vows Is Very Important To God

Ecclesiastes 5:4-6

*"When thou vowest a vow unto God, defer not to pay it. For he hath no pleasure in fools: pay that which thou hast vowed. Better is it that thou shouldest not vow, than that thou shouldest vow and not pay. Suffer not thy mouth to cause thy flesh to sin; neither say thou before the angels, that it was an error: wherefore should God be angry at thy voice, and destroy the works of thine hands?"*

Some may think the main part of the wedding ceremony is the entrance of the bride. Her grand entrance is one of the most anticipated parts of the service, but not the central event. The main component of the wedding ceremony is the exchanging of the vows which finalize the entire ceremony of commitment. We are warned in the word of God against not paying what we have vowed. We are also encouraged to pay that which we have vowed.

Remember, you are committed to what you confess. If you are not sincere about what you're promising, it is better to not promise at all. There are consequences for not keeping the vows. You may be saying, "Boy are you right! Since I got married my life has been turned upside down." You may feel this way, and this may be true, but I'm not talking about the consequences from a horizontal standpoint, I'm speaking of the consequences from a vertical standpoint.

We just read in Ecclesiastes: *why should God be angry at your voice; and destroy the works of your hand.* The reason you have not reached the next plateau in your marriage could be connected to how you are treating your spouse. The reason your business venture was unsuccessful could be tied to the fact that you are not keeping the vows you made. The seasons of your life looked so promising then suddenly, you're faced with uncertainty. Could it be you are not fulfilling what you promised?

Vow making is also important in other aspects of life. In court, we place our hands on the Bible and take an oath to tell the truth. Not just the truth, but the whole truth so help us God. How would you feel if your freedom was at stake? For instance, a witness takes the stand and fails to honor the oath taken. The falsified facts cause you to be sentenced to prison resulting in a loss of freedom, family, and career. Would you be happy with the witness? I doubt it. Would you want to cook for the witness? Hey, be nice! Would you feel love for the witness? The best of us would struggle in this area. Would you want to kiss the witness? Never. Would you vacation with the witness? Of course, you wouldn't. You wouldn't want to have anything to do with the witness because he or she did not keep their word. They broke their vows. As a result, it altered the very course of your life. Well, stop and think. In all honesty this is what we do in our relationships.

To the male reader: You promised to love her, comfort her, honor and keep her in sickness and in health, forsaking all others keeping yourself only unto her, until death do you part. You also promised to have and to hold from this day forward, for better, for worse, for richer for poorer, to love and cherish, till death part the two of you. You said, "I do." You placed a ring on her finger and kissed your bride. It's too late to say, "I don't. Keep the kiss, but give me back the ring." You are committed to what you confessed. You made a commitment and it is your duty and obligation to uphold what you confessed in the sight of God and man. This vow was not for a single act of love, comfort, honor, or faithfulness nor was it a yearly promise, it was a promise for a lifetime.

It is better to not make a vow than to make one and break it. We cannot promise one thing, then render something else. Was the proposal and the wedding a charade? Your wife's desire is to live within the confines of the promises made. News flash! You do not have the right to change the terms of the contract. The man and the woman entered the marriage to perform specific duties and to meet certain obligations. You can't promise to love, then give hatred. You can't promise honor, then give dishonor, disgrace, abuse and shame. You can't promise to cherish then undervalue. You can't promise to comfort, then depress, torture or upset. You do not have the right to change the terms of the contract.

On your wedding day, you were inebriated with love. You must never sober up. You must keep the vow you made. This is the only road to true happiness. Imagine if you will, a marriage restaurant and you are one of the waiters. Your wife is a customer and she look over the menu and places her order. She orders love, honor, cherish, comfort, care, and health. What would you bring her? You will bring her what she ordered! If you don't, she will simply return it. Make sense? Of course, it does! Problems arise in a relationship because we keep delivering what hasn't been ordered. You are the waiter that suggested the entrée. She accepted your recommendation and she deserves the suggested entrée of love and honor to be delivered.

To the female reader: Your vow was the same as your husband's. Just as he is expected to keep and fulfill the duties of the marriage vows, so are you. Remember, your pledge should remain ever before you as well. Your partner should have the confidence that no matter what happens in life or between the two of you, you will always be there rooted, grounded, and committed until death separates the two of you. It's extremely easy to do, but never become too complacent or too comfortable in your relationship. Never take your groom for granted. From time to time, ask yourself if you are delivering what you vowed on your wedding day. You promised to love him, so love him. You promised to honor him, so honor him. You are committed to what you confess. Make the commitment to uphold the vows exchanged on that glorious day.

## Key Points

- Marriage was God's idea. Divorce was man's.

- You are committed to what you confess.

- Remember and deliver the promise of your wedding day.

- Broken vows anger God.

- Your promise contains your spouse's hope and faith.

- Honor your words. Say what you mean and mean what you say.

Death is inevitable. It is a part of the process of life. The love between a man and a woman should be so strong and potent that when death invades their union and takes away the husband or the wife the living spouse is able to declare if they had to do it all over again, they certainly would.

# The Journey Continues...

# Nine

## Say My Name, Say My Name

---

(Gen 3:9) *And the lord God called unto Adam and said where art thou?*

The call of God was two-fold, the call was for his body, more importantly He was summoning his position: leader, ruler and head. God gave Adam a lesson in accountability and Eve a lesson in spousal honor. Honor is the infrastructure or the transportation lines for love.

---

*Disclaimer: In this chapter I am going to rely heavily on the scripture, but it is critical that you read every word to grasp the soundness of what is conveyed.*

What's my name? Notice I did not say, "My name is_____." Legally, to name someone, you must have the authority or be granted permission to do so. In the Bible, names reflected one's character or individuals received their name from any circumstance in their history. Adam's name signifies earth because from the earth he came. Abraham's name means father, Anna means grace, and David means beloved.

When we think about marriage, some couples rarely address each other by their birth name. Almost unconsciously, their spouse's name is replaced with a term of endearment such as sweetheart or darling. It takes the good list as well as the bad list to drive this point home. Millions of couples will address each other by their birth name, but also call each other names based on their actions, lack of action, or apparent character flaw. Sadly, they will call each other stupid, crazy, or ignorant. The list can go on and on.

Most of the time our primary focus is on the person. We deal with the person according to his or her actions. The pivotal point will occur when we learn how to interact with our mate based on their position and not their deeds only.

We are conditioned and trained to respect the president of the United States of America. We respect the office of the president even when the president is behaving non-presidential. The position is worthy of honor and honor should remain regardless of the circumstances. We respect a king, or a judge based upon the title. Even if we disagree with the individual we still respect their status. Wouldn't you agree if you were in the presence of a national leader or the king of a country that you would be on your very best decorum? The same behavior should be applied to our relationships.

If a wife looks upon her husband as only Stanley and not consider his title or the circumstances at hand, her conversation, anger, or bitterness, will be directed toward the husband. If she views him as her king or leader, it will change the entire situation. Allow me to explain. If the wife's reverence is for the head of the household, her leader or king, she will conduct herself differently in his presence. The fact that this leader or king happens to be her husband does not mean he should receive less honor. As a matter of fact, it makes him worthy of double honor. Even though the king and the man are one in the same they should not be treated the same. The king must be honored and respected, even if you want to dishonor and disrespect the man.

Our natural order is to see the man first, then the position of the king or the judge. This must be reversed in marriage. We must retrain ourselves to first see the king or leader, then the man. The same is true concerning the wife. If a husband views his wife as Diana only he will deal with only Diana the wife. If his reverence is for Diana my lady or queen, then he will conduct himself differently in her presence. The wife and the queen are one in the same, yet should not be treated the same. Once again, wouldn't you agree there is a way to address, instruct, disagree, and correct a lady or a queen? Husbands and wives, please understand - regardless of the situation or circumstances, honor should show up first.

The title and position first, then the situation at hand can be dealt with. You can tell him he's wrong, but here's the catch – the key is to tell him he's wrong in the *right* manner. Sarah, whose name means lady gives us an awesome example of honoring a husband. It's ironic that Abraham, who we know as the father of faith, displays (below scripture) a lack of faith which proves we all need time to mature and develop.

Lady: A woman of good family and high social position, a gentlewoman, a woman who is looked up to because she has good taste and pleasant manner. A well-bred woman showing refinement as well as cultivation.

I Peter 3: 1-5

*"Likewise, Ye wives, be in subjection to your own husband; that, if any obey not the word, they also may without the word be won by the conversation of the wives; While they behold your chaste conversation coupled with fear. Whose adorning let it not be that outward adorning of plaiting the hair, and of wearing of gold, or of putting on of apparel; But let it be the hidden man of the heart, in the which is not corruptible, even the ornament of a meek and quiet spirit, which is in the sight of God of great price. For after this manner in the old time the holy women also, who trusted in God, adorned themselves, being in subjection unto their own husbands. Even as Sarah obeyed Abraham, calling him lord: whose daughters ye are, as long as ye do well, and are not afraid with any amazement. "*

What a beautiful passage of scripture. To every woman, God's gift to man, always remember that most men are more interested in your inner beauty rather than your outer beauty. However, men won't complain if you possess both. Outer beauty may attract him, but it may not keep him. I am sure you can think of several high-profile celebrities, for whatever reason, who cannot make a relationship work.

I Peter 3:6

*"Even as Sarah obeyed Abraham, calling him lord: whose daughters ye are, as long as ye do well, and are not afraid with any amazement."*

Like Sarah, who obeyed Abraham and called him lord (her master) you are her daughter if you do what is right and do not give way to fear. Today in marriage, some women are petrified of the word obey. They view it in a negative way instead of a positive way. Please read the verse above again. It says you are Sarah's daughter if you do what's right! What's right is to obey your husband. You cannot be terrified of the word obey and you cannot be afraid to obey. Because of past experiences, many women will get angry if you even *suggest* being obedient to their husband. Anger creates a presence. When a man lives with an angry woman, the existence of her anger is always present to prevent total intimacy. The husband and wife will constantly resist each other until the presence of anger and resentment is eradicated.

Proverbs 21:19

*"It is better to dwell in the wilderness than with a contentious woman."*

It has been said that every woman is not a wife, well every man is not a husband.

1 Peter 3:7

*"Likewise, ye husbands, dwell with them according to knowledge, giving honor unto the wife, as unto the weaker vessel, and as being heirs together of the grace of life; that your prayers be not hindered."*

## Selfsame Love!

Abraham love for Sarai reflects Adam's love for Eve. Abraham love for Sarai and vice versa is simply an extension of the love Adam and Eve shared. Their love (Abraham and Sarai) was also one of sacrifices. The love each couple shared compelled them to protect their union at all cost. As shocking as it may be Adam did not allow his relationship with the creator to come between his relationship with Eve. As you continue to read you will discover that both Abraham and Sarai made enormous sacrifices to protect their union as well. The journey continues!

Abraham was an honorable man. He feared and obeyed God. He was a man of faith. Allow me to bypass the surface and look deeper into Abraham and Sarai's relationship as husband and wife. I believe the reverence and honor Sarai paid to Abraham reflected their public and private life. Marriage is both a public and private affair.

Genesis 12:1-5

*"Now the Lord had said unto Abram, Get thee out of thy kindred, and from thy father's house, unto a land that I will show thee. And I will make of thee a great nation, and I will bless thee, and make thy name great; and thou shalt be a blessing. And I will bless them that bless thee, and curse him that curseth thee: and in thee shall all families of the earth be blessed. So, Abram departed, as the Lord had spoken unto him and Lot went with him: and Abram was seventy and five years old when he departed out of Haran. And Abram took Sarai his wife, and Lot his brother's son,*

*and all their substance that they had gathered, and the souls that they had gotten in Haran; and they went forth to go into the land of Canaan; and into the land of Canaan they came."*

Abraham was instructed by God to leave his kindred, but was not told where he was going. Here is Sarai following her husband in faith as he follows God in faith. As he journeyed, he came across hard times which forced him into Egypt. Abraham, then makes a request of his lady:

Genesis 12:10-20

*"And there was a famine in the land: and Abram went down into Egypt to sojourn there; for the famine was grievous in the land. And it came to pass, when he was come near to enter into Egypt that he said unto Sarai his wife, Behold now, I know that thou art a fair woman to look upon. Therefore, it shall come to pass, when that Egyptians shall say, this is his wife: and they will kill me, but they will save thee alive. Say, I pray thee, thou art my sister: that it may be well with me for thy sake; and my soul shall live because of thee. And it came to pass, that, when Abram was come into Egypt, the Egyptians beheld the woman that she was very fair. The princes also of Pharaoh saw her, and commended her before Pharaoh: and the woman was taken into Pharaoh's house. And he entreated Abram well for her sake: and he had sheep, and oxen, and he asses, and menservants, and maidservants, and she asses, and camels. And the Lord Plagued Pharaoh and his house with great plagues because of Sarai Abram's wife. And Pharaoh called Abram, and said, What is this that thou hast done unto me? Why didst thou not tell me that she was thy wife? Why sadist thou, She is my sister? So, I might have taken her to me to wife: now therefore behold thy wife, take her, and go thy way. And Pharaoh commanded his men concerning him: and they sent him away, and his wife, and all that he had."*

Abraham expressed to his wife that she was a beautiful woman. He communicated and poured his heart out to her. There were no games, lies, half-truths, deception or dishonesty. Most wives will openly express to the husband how much they love, need, treasure, and appreciate them. Overall, men still have a problem in this area. A wife needs to know she's valued as a woman and as a wife. She needs to know she's loved and appreciated not only for what she does, but for who she is.

There are many married men who no longer give their mate a compliment, praise or any type of encouragement or affirmation. They are convinced they no longer need to express to their wife what they feel. Abraham communicated his feelings, desires, fears, and plans to his wife. We need to express, with the mouth, what we feel in the heart. Men, we must open up and share our hopes, fears, frustrations, plans, feelings and desires with our wives. It appears Abraham was selfish in his request, but he really wasn't. Sarai understood his love for her was at the center of his request and reasoning. Sarai also realized Abraham was protecting her as well as himself. Abraham said to her, "When the Egyptian shall see you they shall say this is his wife and they will kill me, but will save you alive."

Abraham did not know whether the fear of God was in Egypt or any other land he traveled to (Genesis 20: 11). That's why he said what he said and did what he did. Sarai was a beautiful and desirable woman. Abraham truly believed they would kill him and save his wife for their pleasure. It's true, he wanted to live, but it's also true, he did not want to see Sarai raped, tortured, or brutalized. He said to her, it might be well with me for thy sake. Abraham needed Sarai and he knew Sarai needed him. This scene repeats it's self again...

Genesis 20:1-7

*"And Abraham journeyed form thence toward the south country and dwelled between Ka'desh and Shur, and sojourned in Ge'-rar. And Abraham said of Sarah his wife, she is my sister: And A-bim'-e-lech king of Ge'rar sent and took Sarah. But God came to A-bim-e-lech in a dream by night, and said to him, Behold, thou art but a dead man, for the woman which thou hast taken: for she is a man's wife. But A-bom-e-lech had not come near her: and he said, Lord, wilt thou slay also a righteous nation? Said he not unto me, She is my sister? And she, even she herself said, He is my brother: in the integrity of my heart and innocence of my hands have I done this. And God said unto him in a dream, Yea, I know that thou didst this in the integrity of thy heart: for I also withheld thee from sinning against me: therefore suffered I thee not to touch her. Now therefore restore the man his wife; for he is a prophet, and he shall pray for thee, and thou shalt live: and if thou restore her not, know thou that thou shalt surely die, thou, and all that are thine."*

So, Sarai is presented to the king who desires her and takes her into his house. Sarai is obeying Abraham her lord and lover. Sarai is simply carrying out the plan. I must admit my amazement here. Sarai remained a lady and would have allowed the King to have sex with her. Not for her sake, but for Abraham's sake. Sarai is willing to sacrifice her body for Abraham. She is willing to be violated by a man she didn't love to protect the man she did love. Let's not forget, Abraham had his own feelings to deal with.

Wait a minute...my wife is in another man's love chamber and he is dimming the lights while preparing to make love to *my* wife, to caress *my* wife, kiss *my* wife, ravish *my* wife, and romance *my* wife. *My God!* I would knock the door down, grab the king, and... Oh, I'm sorry, I'm sorry... this is not *my* story!

Let's continue. Abraham was willing to sacrifice his all-encompassing woman for her sake and his sake. Will we ever be called upon to make such a sacrifice? I hope not, but we can learn a lesson from this. Like Adam and Eve or Abraham and Sarai daily sacrifices are essential. Within the righteous state of marriage when a man and woman live to please each other they will continue to sacrifice their personal desires for their spouse. It took a heavenly intervention to spoil Abraham and Sarai's clever plan. God revealed their secret, yet most of all He kept the king from touching Sarai.

Abraham was able to reach and connect with Sarai because she understood his heart as well as the following.

- Spiritually   He was obeying God

- Personally   She respected him

- Mentally   She understood his reasoning

- Emotionally   He expressed his feelings. Yes, he wanted to live, but wanted to live for her sake also.

- Physically   He wanted to protect her.

- Positional   He was her lord (master)

As we have seen, Abraham made an unusual request of Sarai which she granted. Later in their life, Sarai makes an unusual request of Abraham which he granted. Let's take a further look into the life of Abraham and Sarai's relationship.

Genesis 16:1-6

*"Now Sarai Abram's wife bare him no children: and she has an handmaid, an Egyptian whose name was Hagar. And Sarai said unto Abram, Behold now, the Lord hath restrained me form bearing: I pray thee go in unto my maid, it may be that I may obtain children by her. And Abram hearkened to the voice of Sarai. And Sarai Abram's wife took Hagar her maid the Egyptian, After Abram had dwelt ten years in the land of Canaan, and gave her to*

*her husband Abram to be his wife. And he went in unto Hagar, and she conceived: and when she saw that she had conceived, her mistress was despised in her eyes. And Sarai said unto Abram, My wrong be upon thee: I have given my maid into thy bosom; and when she saw that she had conceived, I was despised in her eyes: the Lord judge between me and thee. But Abram said unto Sarai, Behold, the maid is in thy hand: do to her as it pleaseth thee. And when Sarai dealt hardly with her, she fled from her face."*

Sarai desires to have a child, but her womb is barren. She is not satisfied being barren and she craves and longs to give Abraham a child. She makes a request of her husband to go and have sexual relations with her maidservant. Even though Sarai allows it and Hagar is willing to permit it, Abraham remains the key to producing a child. Sarai needs Abraham's compliance, which he obediently granted.

When a marriage has been inundated with a vast amount of desire to meet each other's needs, the couple will live in a true state of reciprocation. Please do not label the father of faith as a perverted, lustful man.

"What man wouldn't want to have two women?" Is this what you're thinking? Well, there are some men who don't want one-woman moreless two. Who says Abraham was attracted to Hagar or found her desirable? My focus here is Abraham's love and desire to satisfy Sarai's unfulfilled yearning. Remember, she was his lady, his queen, his lover plus Sarai had proven her love for Abraham repeatedly. He is now ready to prove his love for her. Abraham realizes it is not about him, it's all about Sarai and her happiness. For that reason, Abraham consents to his wife's request.

After Hagar conceived a child she began to despise Sarai and Sarai complains. Abraham again desires to please Sarai and informs her that Hagar is in her hands and to do what she thinks is best. His speech and actions are pleasing to the woman he loves.

Throughout her life, Sarai treated Abraham like a king and he treated her like a queen. Regardless of the name your spouse has for you, it should be one of respect and honor.

Consider the following:

*What is my name? I don't complain it's not a bother I am A Father.*

*What is my name? I am your protector, provider, your pleaser, I deserve the honor of A Leader.*

*What is my name? If I hold you in high esteem, kind and not mean I deserve the honor of A King.*

Ladies, when daily honor and respect is given to your leader, king, and father of your children, your marriage will begin to experience tranquility as you settle into the God state of matrimony.

*What's my name? I gave birth to your children, I am like no other I am a Mother.*

*What's my name? I made a commitment, a pledge for life I deserve the honor of a Wife.*

*What's my name? I respect you like a father, honor you like a priest serve you like a king I am your Queen.*

*What's my name? I'm your sweetheart, honey, and baby I'm your Phenomenal Lady.*

Gentlemen, when daily honor and respect is bestowed on your wife, lady, queen, and the mother of your children, your relationship will reach a plateau another can only dream about.

As Abraham and Sarai traveled, Sarai could have gone off on Abraham telling him what she was and wasn't going to do. Sarai had a choice in the matter. She could have told Abraham, "Oh no, buddy! Be a man, half of the truth is a whole lie. I don't want anything to do with your plan." Thank God, she didn't. In your relationship, honor must be a high priority. It is a key ingredient to produce a happy marriage. Honor determines not only what we do, but it determines *how* we do it as well. It not only determines what we say, but also *how* we say it. Regardless of the situation or circumstances, honor should show up first, first in the title and position, then the situation at hand can be dealt with. It's telling him he's wrong, but again, the catch is telling him he's wrong in the right manner.

## Key Points

- Treat your spouse like royalty to be treated like royalty.

- Someone must lead, and someone must follow.

- Honor in a relationship leaves no room for intimidation, domination, or manipulation.

- There are times when you must submit your will and your body for the good of the relationship.

- There are times you will find it necessary to go along to get along.

- In the life of others, be prepared to sow the same blessing you reap.

- When a marriage has been inundated with a vast amount of desire to meet each other's needs, the couple will live in a true state of reciprocation.

# The Journey Continues...

# Ten

## SEASONAL EXPRESSIONS OF LOVE

---

Change is inevitable: The first couple, the couple that God HIMSELF married, had to cope with changing times. Prepare yourself because nothing stays the same. Every relationship will experience changing times as well. Changing seasons are a part of life.

---

Because of the wonderment nature invites, I sometimes stop and think how amazing it is to be alive. To feel the summer breeze, to watch the birds fly, or to absorb the warmth of the sun on a beautiful summer day is remarkable. Things are changing all around us and these changes are a sign of life. Each season ushers in its own set of challenges and require us to adjust to the season. The seasons of life do not adjust to us, we adjust to the seasons of life. When it's cold, we put on a coat. When it's hot we will remove the coat. I love nature and how the seasons automatically change. Nature has certainly taught me a lot about life. Life has its seasons and your marriage is no exception - it will go through seasonal changes. It is an acceptable fact of life that everything changes; nothing stays the same.

There are things you can do and experience in one season that you probably cannot do and experience in another. Let's explore marriage as it alters from season to season. Not the seasons of nature, but the symbolic seasons of your marriage. To prepare, survive, and enjoy the seasons of marriage, every couple requires a working knowledge of what to expect in the various seasons. Understanding the seasonal changes is like understanding how to read a map. Without such knowledge, a couple places themselves at a great disadvantage.

Knowing where you are must be as equally important as knowing where you're going; if you do not know where you are, it's possible to end up somewhere else. It has been said that every journey begins with a step, so let's begin our journey through the seasonal expressions of love in marriage and understand where we are and where we may be headed.

## Spring

Nature awakens in spring. Flowers are blooming, and everything is coming back to life. The cold, harsh winter months are over. This is a time to rejoice! As nature awakens, so does the spirit of the people. When we think of spring we think of newness and new beginnings. What an exciting period.

## Spring In Marriage

Every relationship experiences spring. Spring in our relationship is the early period of love as well as the early stages of marriage. Everything is budding and blossoming. Love is wonderful, fresh, new, and exciting. This is a special time in marriage. Just as spring melts away the snow, spring time in marriage melts away faults, anger, resentment, frustration, and criticism. We warm up quickly to the desires and needs of one another. We are open and excited about each other's hopes and dreams. Everything is awakening including finances and careers. You may even think it doesn't get any better than this. "Boy, if I knew marriage was going to be this good I would have married a long time ago!"

What an exciting period. You wish it could last forever and it appears to be doing just that. It's getting better because spring turns into summertime. Before we look at summertime in marriage, let's first look at the season of summer.

## Summer

Summertime is the warmest season of the year or should I say the hottest season. It is extremely necessary that one learn how to survive by staying cool during the hot summer months. It is a season of refreshing as well as fun and games.

## Summer In Marriage

As spring comes to an end in your relationship, the two of you are now more familiar with one another than ever before. The newness and the freshness are beginning to fade, yet after all this time there is still so much love and happiness. Things are hot between the two of you. You're on fire, burning up with love and passion. Sex is the best that it has ever been. You simply can't keep your hands off each other. Throughout the day you are thinking about and calling each other every chance you get. Your social life is off the radar. You enjoy going out and doing things with other couples. You take pleasure in being around family and friends. Life is good!

## Summertime In Your Finances:

1. You are purchasing new homes, cars, clothes and jewelry
2. No need to budget or watch your spending
3. Two or three vacations per year.
4. Carefree with money
5. Two income family - financial future looks bright

Warning: During the four seasons the sun still lights the day, the moon and stars light the night, oxygen still fills the atmosphere, dew continues to fall, and it continues to rain. News Flash! The same is also true for your marriage. Financial commitments and obligations will remain in every marital season. You will need an income for food, clothing, and shelter. The money will be needed for insurance, taxes, utilities, and emergencies.

Out of the four seasons, summer and winter are the two deadliest or dangerous season for humans. Both seasons provide many opportunities for pleasure, enjoyment, as well as excitement, but it does not negate the following:

## Summer

1. Hundreds drown worldwide from water activities.
2. Thousands suffer from heat exhaustion and heat strokes due to exposure to the sun.
3. The Gulf Coast experiences hurricane season.
4. Various natural disasters occur in the summer months.
5. More automobile deaths occur due to increased highway traffic.
6. Thousands of accidental injuries and deaths occur due to summer activities.

## Winter

1. Thousands of deaths associated with freezing temperature.
2. Heater fires and Carbon monoxide poisoning occur while attempting to stay warm.
3. Various natural disasters occur during in the winter months.
4. Thousands of accidental injuries and deaths occur due to winter activities.

When it comes to your relationship, summer and winter are also the two deadliest or dangerous seasons in marriage. When your relationship is in summer time things are hot, exciting, and everything appears to be going your way. However, hot is one thing… boiling over is another. The danger for couples is over-heating. Just as you must protect yourself from over-heating physically, you must, at all costs, protect your relationship and finances from overheating. You must go through this season with precaution because this season has the potential of continual success or a set up for potential failure. Don't be misguided by the fact that the future looks bright and the two of you are extremely happy.

Red alert: Couples need to learn how to live and survive in the summer of their relationship. Protection against over-heating should be your major concern. Be careful, because you can say where you have been, but you can't say where you are going.

## Lessons Against Over-Heating

- The good times may not last forever

- Watch your spending, establish spending limits

- Have a plan for your life and finances

- Take your eyes off the Joneses

- Love making may be hot, but even this should be practiced in moderation. No one needs to make love seven times a day, seven days a week.

- With the proper planning and precaution, it is possible to spend the life of your marriage in this season.

- Spring or summer is the ideal season to live in although spring is almost impossible for most couples.

- It is what you do in the summer that prevents fall from coming.

- Regardless of where your marital season starts the order of the seasons is still winter, spring, summer, and fall.

- Your relationship has gone from spring to summer. Do everything within your power to stay in one of these seasons of love because the next season is fall.

## Fall

The time of falling leaves and harvest time for many crops. Days are warm. Nights are cool as winter approaches. The wind becomes chilly and frost often occurs at night. The summer heat gives way to the lightly cooler temperatures. Every marriage will not go through the season of fall nor is it necessary that they do. Fall is the season where it appears everything is falling apart. It is getting more and more difficult to maintain all the intricacies of your relationship. A job loss, sickness, pregnancy, emergency, or a natural disaster can create havoc for an unsuspecting couple.

## In The Fall

- Financial stability has been replaced with financial uncertainty.
- The positive future forecast looks hazy.
- Overheating is no longer a possibility.

The effects of the lack of finances are beginning to show. You have noticed your lovemaking is cooling off as well. Several times a day has been replaced with seven times a month. You are discovering - no finance no romance. You're wondering what's happening as your desire to please each other slowly dwindles. The communication between the two of you is at an all - time low.

Fall is harvest time for many crops and can be harvest time for your relationship. There are some mental positives you planted in the previous seasons like savings, investing, wise spending, quality time with each other, moderation in lovemaking, and good communication skills. Your harvest may not be plentiful, but gather and preserve all you can. The gathered harvest, if built upon, will strengthen and help you reclaim the season of summer or maintain the best parts of fall.

Fall is a crucial season for couples. Unlike nature, you can reverse this season of your marriage. Your relationship needs an examination, so take a serious look at every aspect of your relationship. Failure to be honest and confront the serious issues will not help the relationship or equip the two of you with the necessary tools to vacate this unwarranted season. If you don't maintain or reverse the fall season of your relationship, winter is clearly around the corner. The closer you get to winter the more things will chill. The relationship will not only become chilly, frost in addition to snow may be in your forecast.

## SPRING MAY TURN TO SUMMER

## SUMMER MAY TURN TO FALL

## FALL MAY TURN TO WINTER

Winter: The coldest season of the year. Winter is the one season you want to prevent your relationship from entering. You want to avoid this season at all costs. Winter could bring the death of your marriage. Coldness and frost are the order of the day. Your marriage will experience frost emotionally, physically, and spiritually. Coldness will rule the day as well as the night.

The difference between nature winter and relationship winter is the length of the season. Nature winter normally will last three to four months. Relationship winter can last three to four months or three to four years or even longer depending upon the incidences. How will you know your relationship is in the winter months? The answer is simple. When everything is cold and very cold between the two of you.

| Winter time for the Husband | Winter time for the Wife |
|---|---|
| ◆ She looks at you and rolls her eyes for no apparent reason.<br><br>◆ She comes to bed dressed like a mummy.<br><br>◆ You arrive home from work and all your belongings are on the front lawn.<br><br>◆ She has not cooked in a month and you haven't asked why.<br><br>◆ Her facial expression is killing you on the inside.<br><br>◆ She is eating an apple when you are having sex.<br><br>◆ You're having sex and she's one hundred percent silent.<br><br>◆ When or if you stop breathing; your wife finishes getting dressed and drives to work to call 911.<br><br>◆ She cooked your favorite meal and you are afraid to eat it. | ◆ When you are begging him to make love to you.<br><br>◆ You have not had sex in a month, you are wearing your sexy lingerie and he falls asleep or his Viagra failed.<br><br>◆ You are choking to death and he's offering you something to eat.<br><br>◆ When jail is better than home.<br><br>◆ You are packing your suitcase to leave him and he helps you pack.<br><br>◆ When he gives you the name of the other women he's interested in.<br><br>◆ He calls 911 on you.<br><br>◆ You cooked his favorite meal, prepared a candle light dinner and he left home.<br><br>◆ When he has more time for others than for you. |

Winter should be avoided at all costs. It will take knowledge, wisdom, and patience to break out of it. Your present and future state of marriage may look grim, nonetheless there is hope. Spring time can melt away the ice and remove the emotional frost that has settled upon the two of you.

Chapter seven is the twin chapter to this one. Please apply the lessons learned in both chapters to take your relationship to new heights. Yes, my friend, spring will follow winter, but if possible, avoid the coldness, dreariness, and frost of winter. Every serious relationship is traveling at its own rate of speed. It doesn't matter if we are talking about several days or several years. Before a relationship ends, it must go through the four seasons.

## Key Points

- The symbolic seasons of your marriage are winter, spring, summer, and fall.

- Spring is a wonderful season filled with newness and freshness.

- Summer is the hottest season. Couples should protect themselves against overheating.

- Fall is the cooling off period. Mistakes and unwise decisions produce this season.

- Winter is the coldest season. Avoid winter at all costs. Divorce is a real possibility.

- Nothing stays the same; you can count on it. The season of your marriage will change.

- Summer and winter are the two deadliest seasons for your marriage.

# The Journey Continues...

# Eleven

# LOVING WITHOUT WORDS

The language of silence. For the most part, Adam and Eve loved each other without words. Loving without words doesn't mean words are never spoken, it simply means the spoken word does not dominate the situation at hand. Sometimes, like Adam and Eve, words can hinder the healing process because the ocean of love is deep and wide.

Speech is a wonderful thing, Speech allows us to communicate with one another and express the sentiments of our heart. Speech allows us to express an array of emotions such as love, excitement, and joy just to name a few. The focal point of this chapter is not the emotions which strain our relationship. You know, the negative ones so easily displayed like anger, resentment, bitterness and hostility. The design of this chapter is to deepen the emotional and physical bond between you and your mate by encouraging a nonverbal form of communication to express love, tenderness, pleasure, joy and excitement. Verbal communication can sometimes get in the way of the message. We know exactly what we are trying to express, but for some unknown reason the wrong words, tone, look or jester keeps getting in the way. We're conversing but the conversation lacks flow. We are dealing with conversation word block - words are getting in the way of the sincere expression. When words, tone, looks or negative jesters get in the way, our arguments are prolonged, apologies rejected, voices elevated, and intimacy is evaporated.

We are no longer communicating; we are sparring. Verbal sparring is a battle of the wits. There was a time in my relationship when communication between my wife and I was at an all-time low. Our attempts to communicate would turn into sparring sessions which turned into verbal boxing matches.

With a term of endearment, she would approach me and say, "Baby, we need to talk." In my mind, I heard ring the bell here we go. Sure enough, we would start out talking like we always do, but five minutes into the conversation one of us would start putting on the gloves. We weren't communicating, it was just a battle of wits.

I wanted more. I wanted to reconnect with the woman I married, but how? We were fighting, but we weren't fighting for the same (prize, reward) thing. She was fighting to connect emotionally, and I was fighting to connect physically.

Understanding what was happening to us allowed us to channel our negative emotions and combative nature. Valuable lessons were also learned because of the struggle. Lessons that strengthened our union and restored the emotional as well as the physical closeness between us. Your marriage will benefit from these lessons immensely.

Love is like an ocean and the ocean of love is very deep. Most couples have not even started to explore the deepness of their love. To help you understand this aspect of love, realize that love can be expressed shallowly, or love can be expressed deeply. A shallow expression of love is like learning how to swim in shallow water. Learning how to swim requires the emergence of one's body into the water. Although frightening at first, shallow water must be exchanged for deeper water. The depth of the water allows the external extremities to have full motion or range while in the water. Love is no different. Maturing your love requires that you submerge yourself emotionally into the soul of your significant other.

I hear you! I hear you saying, "I'm afraid to do that." For a plethora of reasons, fear will prevent you from doing the very thing that will deepen the emotional bond between the two of you. Only change can produce the change you so desperately seek in your relationship. Believe it or not, shallow sharing stifles intimacy and love. This writing is for those who have a sincere desire to fix what's ailing their marriage.

Every married couple should be striving for a deeper level of emotional and physical intimacy. Coexisting is not enough. You must strive to go deep inside the core of your mate. Keep in mind, the origin of physical depth and emotional depth are the same. Both are achieved through the process of choosing. Physical depth is representative of one's choice to freely give one flesh/body to another. Emotional depth is representative of one's choice to give one soul or life for another.

Physical depth connects flesh to flesh. Emotional depth connects one soul to the soul of another. Why are there so many problems in relationships? Notice I did not say marriage, I said relationships; however, a relationship does encompass marriage. This question has already been answered, but I will explore it deeper. The answer is contained in my previous quote of, "She was fighting to connect emotionally, and I was fighting to connect physically."

The problem exists because one mate is desiring physical depth, while the other mate is desiring emotional depth. More times than not this is the culprit. I'll make it a little more personal - Most men desire physical (SEX) depth. Most women desire emotional (mental connection) depth. What's the problem? The problem is the intertwining of their diametric mindsets; therefore, the quest for what is lacking or incompatible.

## THE COMPATIBILITY LANDSCAPE

The pursuit for compatibility is not a utopian state, rather it is a harmonious state of coexisting with your significant other. A study of the table below reveals we are the happiest when we are matched with an equal counterpart. The table will also show that we are the most unfulfilled when we are matched with a non-equal counterpart.

| MAN | WOMAN |
| --- | --- |
| Physical depth | Physical depth |
| Emotional depth | Emotional depth |
| Physical depth | Emotional depth |
| Emotional depth | Physical depth |
| Physical Emotional | Physical Emotional |

Remember, the quest is for compatibility. As you can see, from the chart above, compatibility can be discovered in many various combinations. Now, let's look at the essence of what is proposed. Regardless of how long you may have been married, every couple's relationship is operating under the proposed:

### Physical Depth-Physical Depth

In marriage, physical to physical does not mean the relationship is void of emotion, it simply means that the physical dominates. It means emotion does not prevent nor hinder the two of them from coming together in an all-out sexual manner.

These couples can press beyond the emotional to achieve the physical. They enjoy sex and the gambit of their sexual exploits can range from A-Z. I am not endorsing anything here, I am simply pointing out the strong sexual desire to physically satisfy each other. Most couples who reside here will place no limits on what they will or will not do in the bedroom. The physical aspect of their relationship allows them to go deep in their expression of love. Right or wrong, like a sacrificial lamb, they offer themselves to each other. Sex is an offering of self for the consensual fulfillment of the other.

To take this a step further, it (physical to physical) is a pulsating craving within the flesh that's compelling him or her to do whatever. Right or wrong, this is the reality of their depth. These couples are indeed happy, but there is a deeper level of depth to be gained.

Outside of marriage, the physical to physical IS ALL ABOUT THE PHYSICAL. It has nothing to do with commitment, love, care, or concern; it's all about the flesh. It's about getting each other off, so to say. The porn industry and those who engage in prostitution prove this to be true. It's not about love, it's about the flesh and the mighty dollar.

If the price is right, a woman or a man will allow another to use his or her flesh to satisfy whatever deep, abnormal, odd, or freakish fetish he or she may have. More times than not it is the female allowing the male to indulge himself with her body.

## Emotional Depth - Emotional Depth

In like manner to the above, emotional to emotional depth does not mean the relationship is void of physical depth or physical contact like kissing, hugging, cuddling, or holding hands. In this case, it simply means that the emotional dominates. On the other hand, due to age, sickness, or some other condition, deep physical expression may not be possible or warranted. The connection the two share supersedes being sexually intimate with one another. When an emotionally driven man connects with an emotionally driven woman, wholeness is derived from and through the emotional connection shared. Like an umbilical cord, the emotional portal connects the two allowing the (deep feeling) soulfulness to pass through.

Age and maturity play a major role in reaching this level of depth. For some reason, it eludes the young and foolish at heart simply because women pursue the emotional while their male counterparts are pursuing the physical. Between the emotional and the physical, there is no battle for supremacy. It is the emotional connection that assures the bond and produces the happiness.

## Physical Depth - Emotional Depth

This is the place of contention, frustration, strife and numerous arguments. This depth is the reason for most divorces. Most marriages reside here. The first noticeable thing should be the incompatibility. One desires the physical and the other desires the emotional. In the eyes of these couples, their unmet expectation is the hindrance to marital bliss. The couple loves each other, but are not fully satisfied with each other. Neither is totally getting what he or she needs or desires from the other. The man craves more of the sexual depth and the woman craves more emotional depth, although more women today are embracing their sexuality and some desire sex more than the man.

When the physical live with the emotional the battle is for supremacy. He or she is constantly attempting to get the other to adjust themselves to their liking. The verbal argument is: if you do ABC, then I'll do DEF. Back and forth they go to no avail. After a while and like a volcano, the toxins build up unmet expectations, erupts spewing ashes of anger, bitterness, resentment, frustration and regrets. Like the mouth of a volcano, there's a gaping hole in the relationship which I will address later in this chapter. To curb the anxiety, and for the good of the union one or both must shift mentally.

## Physical/Emotional - Physical/Emotional

The happiest couples are the ones that are meeting both the physical and emotional needs of each other. Our Lord and Savior, Jesus Christ said, *"Give and ye shall receive."* Giving and receiving is reciprocal. It does not mean if you go deep in an area (sexual act) that he or she will go deep with you in that same area. It is not tit for tat. It is having a sincere desire to meet and satisfy the emotional and physical needs of each other. Once again, the depth of what is given (individual act or action) does not always determine the depth of what one will receive. Unlike giving to the Lord, which contains a spiritual (increase) component, the reciprocal and depending upon what's desired, emotional or physically from him or her, maybe more or less.

Dislikes and displeasures do exist within these relationships. It is the overall state of the union that catapults these couples to the place of happiness. They enjoy sex and the gambit of their sexual exploits can range from A-Z. They give themselves to each other lovingly and freely. Also, and as previously stated, they have the emotional portal which connects the two in a deep-seated way. The intensity of love is measured by the degree of one's love for another. The extent of love is measured by depth and determines how far (deep) one is willing to go to connect with another.

## The Intensity Of Love

Once again, the intensity of love is determined by the temperature of one's love which determines what one gives or sacrifices for another. The following true story will help me drive this point home. One day a friend of mine, whom we'll call Bob, called me with concerns about a mutual friend, whom we will call Ted. Ted is the ideal husband. The kind of man that most women dream about. He's handsome, hardworking, faithful, spiritual and lovingly committed to his wife, yet his marriage is in crises. The problem that's plaguing his marriage is one that's so familiar - the forbidden fruit. Ted is dealing with the second episode of betrayal and infidelity in his marriage. Not only is he dealing with betrayal, but he's dealing with the pain of hearing his wife on the phone confess her love to another man. If that wasn't enough, Ted has also miserably listened to his wife express her disdain for him. In silence, he listens as his wife discusses leaving him for the other man. In disbelief and with tears streaming down his face, he cringes as she voices her amazement at the size of her lover's anatomy which she claimed thrilled her beyond her wildest dreams. Sitting in a well-lit room, but mentally in a dark place, he continues to listen as his wife boasts about her ability to perform oral sex and her first-time anal act. Stripped of his manhood, he continues to listen as the love birds are making plans for their next sexual excursion.

To the male reader, I hear you. Yes, Ted's wife is still alive. Ted was not only listening, but he was recording the conversation. In haste and heartbroken, he confronts the wife with the undeniable, excruciating evidence. While on the phone talking to me, Bob is livid because the shocking part of the story was still to come. Ted did not pack his bags, he didn't leave, break anything, grab her by the throat, swear, nor threaten her with violence. With sorrow in his heart, this broken man stood there confessing his undying love to the woman who has just shattered his world. To no avail, he pleads with her to leave her lover and for the two of them to seek counseling which she objected to.

Like a wailing dog bewildered and outdone, Bob howls into the air, "WHAT'S WRONG WITH HIM?" Not at a loss for words, I commenced to share the following with my bewildered friend. Although a lesson was learned that day, it did not change how Bob felt about Ted's situation. You see, Bob did not view Ted as a sympathetic victim. To the contrary, Bob viewed Ted as the fool of all fools. Nonetheless, I explained to Bob that Ted was loving at a different Celsius degree - at another *heat* (degree) level. Ted's love is more intensified. Not that I am comparing Ted to God, but he is loving in a higher manner.

John 3:16
*"For God so loved the world that he gave his only begotten Son...*

For God *sooooo* loved the world to the greatest degree that he gave his only begotten son - the greatest gift. The degree of love will always determine how one responds to the object of his/her love. Also, the degree of love is determined by how far one is willing to go to express their love as well as the personal price they're willing to pay for his or her love. In the heart of mankind, love operates like a thermostat. We all love, but to a different degree. The greater the degree the greater the sacrifice. So, as painful as it was for Ted, Ted could not let his wife go. As of this writing, Ted and his wife are *still* together.

Once again, the design of this chapter is to deepen the emotional and physical bond between you and your mate by encouraging a nonverbal form of communication to express love, tenderness, pleasure, joy and excitement. As previously stated, verbal communication can sometimes get in the way of the message. We know exactly what we are trying to express, but for some unknown reason the wrong words, tone, look or jester keeps getting in the way. Words are, without a doubt, our greatest form of communication, spoken or written, but in the confines of marriage words *sometimes* get in the way.

Would you agree that not everyone can be a spokesperson, an advocate who speaks on behalf of another? It's not wise to send just anyone out to represent you or your company, especially during claims of financial liability, facing criminal charges or if your reputation is on the line. When a spokesperson is required, and if given a choice, most will send one that is knowledgeable, smart, intelligent, and articulate in speech. Some people need a spokesperson because every time they open their mouth, stupidity jumps out, they inflict pain, incriminate themselves or worsen the situation. Every day in the world of marriage, this is exactly what's happening. Unlike the spokesperson who is used by a corporation, husbands and wives represent themselves. Remember, everyone is not a good spokesperson.

When one's own verbal communication becomes disruptive or damaging to the relationship, another form of communication is needed. The primary method of communicating is speech and the secondary are expressive writing. The proposed (nonverbal communication) is for lovers only and should be used in the confines of a loving, caring relationship. It is for those desiring a deeper level of physical intimacy and the burning intensity that locks two souls together.

## Without Words

Nonverbal communication may initially pull you out of character and you may even feel a little foolish, but if you stay with it, it will work wonders for your sex life. I truly believe the sound of love should be joyous, and the scent of love should be pleasant like the dawning of a new day. The taste of love should be sweet, the touch of love should be soft, and the sight of love should be pleasing. Communicating without words is more than body language, it is learning how to express oneself without the use of words. It's using your God given features, attributes, and gifting to express love, desire, tenderness, plus care and concern.

I will admit that women are better at this than men, and have far more tools to utilize the suggested, but men can learn nonverbal as well. The following is to whet your appetite for the nonverbal form of communication and, on your own accord, explore the subject matter more in-depth.

## The Power In Non-Verbal

**Embrace:** A close affectionate and protective acceptance. To embrace is different from hugging. Although both contain an affectionate quality, it is the protective quality of the embrace that separates the two. When insecurity and rejection creep into your relationship, the utilization of a sincere embrace will transmit security, safety and protection.

**Hug or Hugging:** To squeeze tightly in your arms usually with fondness and affectionate play. A suggestion to the male: create a light hearted or feel good moment without saying a word. While standing behind your wife, take her in your arms and tightly squeeze her. The position in which the two of you are hugging relaxes the female and encourages affectionate play.

**Eyesight:** The faculty of vision. Eye to eye contact is a great way to connect with your wife whether standing, sitting, or lying down. The intriguing look of the observer is titillating to the one being observed. To send a strong message of importance, pierce long and hard into his or her eyes as if you were attempting to look deep inside their soul.

**Smile:** A facial expression characterized by turning up the corners of the mouth. Usually shows pleasure, satisfaction, or amusement. Nothing expresses pleasure like a smile. The captured smile signals pleasure, warmth, joy, excitement and happiness. Smile during your conversations or when being addressed, and at all costs, smile often during your time of lovemaking.

**Touch:** The act of contacting with another. Touching allows us to bond with another. A single touch sends emotional signals throughout the body. Touching has been called the feel-good energy. There's a medicinal effect assorted with touching. A touch has the power to heal, connect, and nourish physically as well as emotionally. The right touch at the right time will work wonders in your relationship. Stop talking and start touching. In marriage, hug, hold hands, cuddle and massage, comb his/her hair, shower together, grab him/her, play footsie, horseplay, etc. Even when things are somewhat bad between the two of you and you find yourself dealing with anger, bitterness and coldness, remember a properly placed touch can restore the unity.

**Ear:** The organ for hearing. When communication deteriorates the volume escalates. In dealing with one another, we start talking louder to be heard. When you refuse to give an ear, you are sending the message that he/she is unimportant. Listening reflects care and concern; therefore, when your significant other is addressing you, the following will be helpful to send a strong message of attentiveness: 1. Lean toward him or her. 2. Tilt your head to one side or the other. 3. Nod your head back and forth two or three times.

**Nose:** The organ of smell and entrance to the respiratory tract. In general, we love it when others take notice of a certain perfume or cologne we may be wearing and it's no different in marriage. Your sensory receptor can be used to satisfy your mate in a special way as well. Standing near or while the two of you are embracing, inhale deeply then sigh (hum). The nose is a symbol of inquisitiveness. Without words, continue to sniff his or her clothing, neck, or other areas assorted with the pleasant aroma. Brothers, your sensory receptor will serve you well here. After she's taken her bath, you know the one with the mixture of oils, scented soaps, perfumes, body gels, and tantalizing bath bubbles. Approach her and inhale *her* and simply hum!

**Lips:** You can use the lips to nibble on the ear, you can perch your lips like a kiss with a seductive look in your eyes, you can lick your lips, you can use your lips to kiss softly and gently all over his/her body, you can leave lip print notes, and even mouth I love you to him or her.

## Key Points

- Coexisting is not enough.

- There's a power in the non-verbal.

- Verbal sparring is a battle of the wits.

- Compatibility is a harmonious state of coexisting with your significant other.

- The degree of love determines what one is willing to give.

- Words sometimes get in the way of the expressive.

- Love can be expressed through the verbal and the non-verbal

# The Journey Continues...

# Twelve

## GETTING TO KNOW YOU

> Self-belief is blinding. In the garden, the mother of all living, (Eve) *failed to realize* that she didn't know herself as well as she thought; therefore, she was blind-sided by the serpent. The enemy will always use your lack of self-knowledge against you. It's good to know your partner, it's better to know your Self.

In marriage, we spend so much of our time and efforts acquiring spousal information that we have not taken the time to truly know ourselves. Our focus has been their likes, dislikes, needs and desires. We have placed so much effort on learning how to live as a cohesive unit until we've gotten lost in the process. Some spouses will boldly declare they know their mate better than they know themselves. I always find that comment astonishing because each life is a lifetime of discovery.

One will not know all there is to know about their *self* before exiting this world. This assumption of knowing one better than one knows themselves is based upon our thinking process. We feel we understand and know the other person because we are acquitted with their ways. This does not constitute or give us the right to formulate such a belief.

Knowing a person's likes and dislikes gives us insight into their character and may even make them predictable. Nevertheless, this cannot be construed or confused with having full knowledge about an individual. In most cases, not all, we can predict with a degree of certainty what they will or will not do. Someone can report something about your spouse and you will receive or reject this information based on the character knowledge you have of them. It is a wonderful thing to be connected in such a strong way to your mate. This strong connection has been transmitted by communication, observance, and time. Knowing your partner is great; however, the question is how well do you know yourself? In marriage, it is central that we know and understand ourselves to have our needs and desires met. I can't be all that I can be until I first confront me, know me, understand me, and if necessary change me.

We spend our time constantly seeking to change our spouse, but what if the problem is not with our spouse? What if the problem is with me or you? *GASP!* Shocking, I know! For the most part, when we think of problems it is always the other individual that has them. The reason is undoubtedly clear, the eye is designed to look outward, so it's easy for you to see me, my mistake, faults, shortcomings, and any other character deficiencies I may have. Have you noticed how quickly we can see others in a negative light and see ourselves in a positive light?

This may sound like a ridiculous question, but I must ask it anyway. If you had to live with a replica of you, would you find living with them exciting, fun, stimulating, and enjoyable? If you wouldn't be happy living with a replica of you, why should your mate be happy living with you? Do you have a passion for life or are you simply talking about life's passions? Some individuals are on the conversational road of life not the achievement road. They are always talking about the things they desire to do or change, but never put forth a real effort to accomplish such things. Are you simply having a conversation about a better marriage? Are you doing the things that will produce a better marriage? You can't just talk about it, you must be about it! Being able to answer these questions and knowing yourself is the only way to achieve your heart's desires.

| Talking About It | But Never |
|---|---|
| Your desire for closeness | Doing the things that produce closeness |
| Desire for quality time | Creating quality time |
| Desire for intimacy | Planning for intimacy |
| Desire for love, sex and romance | Putting forth an effort |
| Changing career | Seeking to educate yourself |

Knowing some things about your Self is different from discovering some things about your Self. You possess some qualities and strengths that you yourself do not even realize. These abilities as well as inabilities are lying dormant awaiting your recognition and command. It is easy for one to speak of strength when strength from within is not called upon. It is easy for one to speak of faith when their faith is not summoned to produce a result. What will you say? What will you do? When the things you discover about yourself surprise even you.

How well do you know your Self? The questions below are designed to stimulate and challenge your thoughts concerning you. You may discover or uncover some underlying fears, phobias, inhibitions, desires, suspicions, worries, or weaknesses. These thought-provoking questions may enable you to see that more time and energy should be invested in confronting all the issues related to your Self. Most of your answers could be followed up with a why or why not.

## Life Questions

1. Why are you here?

2. What is your purpose in life?

3. Have you discovered the meaning of life?

4. Where are you going (destiny)?

5. Are you making a difference in your community, society?

6. Are you making the most of your time here on Earth?

7. What are some of the things you regret?

8. Who will mourn you when you are gone?

9. What is your greatest fear?

10. If you are not perfect, what is wrong with you?

11. Why are you convinced there's life after death?

12. If you discovered you were adopted, would it change the love you have for the family that reared you?

13. If you held the cure to all diseases, but couldn't profit financially, would you give the cure to the world?

## Personal Questions

1. Are you happy?

2. Are you judgmental?

3. Are you in love?

4. Are you mentally free?

5. What or who is hindering you?

6. Are you fearful?

7. Are you trustworthy?

8. Is there anyone that you hate?

9. Is your love tank full or empty?

10. Are you healed from the past or hurting from the past?

11. Do you like yourself?

12. Are you selfish?

13. Are you enjoyable to be around?

14. Are you kind and considerate?

15. Are you really a Christian?

16. Are you optimistic?

17. Are you pessimistic?

18. Is it fun to be with you?

19. Are you a private person?

20. Are you confrontational?

## Relationship Questions

1.  Do you enjoy being married?

2.  Do you really love your spouse?

3.  Deep down do you want a divorce?

4.  Would you marry him or her again?

5.  Are you emotionally happy?

6.  Is this relationship meeting all your needs?

7.  Are you satisfied with your love life?

8.  Do you enjoy communicating with him or her?

9.  What is the best thing about your relationship?

10. What do you like most about yourself?

11. What do you dislike the most about yourself?

12. Do you feel fulfilled?

13. What is the worst thing about your marriage?

14. What is the best thing about your marriage?

15. Are your best years together beyond you or before you?

## Tough Personal Questions

1. What if you discovered your religion was wrong? Would you alter the rest of your life?

2. If you are right 80% of the time, what damage are you inflicting with being wrong 20% of the time?

3. Who are you making miserable or unhappy?

4. Who loves you enough to die for you?

5. Who are you willing to die for?

6. Would you steal to satisfy a hunger?

7. If your husband's brother, or your wife's sister had sexual desires toward you, would you cross that line, keep it a secret, or reveal it?

8. Have you truly forgiven those who have wounded you?

9. Are you as innocent as you represent or proclaim?

10. What is ugly on the inside of you?

11. How many people are sleeping in your bed?

12. While you are making love to your spouse has anyone else ever crossed your mind?

This is worth repeating: marriage is about finding the right person, but more importantly, it is about being the right person. When the two of you first met the worst of you were indeed hidden. In our everyday life, it's easy to lose sight of being the right person. We now offer our mate the worst of ourselves than adopt an attitude of

*I am just being myself.* Never forget marriage is as much about being the right person as it is finding the right person. Concerning most disagreements, the husband and the wife's normal response is...*if they would do this I would do that.* You will never maximize your relationship by reacting only to what your spouse does or doesn't do.

Over the years, I've heard many people make the comment about being sick and tired. Sick and tired is not enough. It's vital for you to be proactive and not reactive only. You must take control of your own actions, thereby strengthening the bonds of your union. Knowing what to do and doing what you know is not the same. Be honest with yourself to accomplish your dreams and goals. Lip service must confront genuine effort. If it is not coming from the heart, then it is vain. Lip service could be dominating your heart service.

## Problems In Marriage

Things are not always as they appear. Do you look outwardly before you look inwardly without complete knowledge or seeking information? Just looking at a situation could cause you to make an error in judgment. Part of the facts or part of the truth could be more damaging than none of the truth. The reason why this is true is that the mind will automatically seek to fill in the missing unknown factors.

Problems *will* arise in your marriage. There are some situations you will never resolve or some problems you will never solve looking only inwardly or outwardly. Looking inward or outward only has the potential to mislead you. You must learn to reach upward to the source for clear and concise resolution. Question – who is the source? Answer - The origin of the problem. In other words, if I created a problem for you, you will never be able to solve the complete problem using your own reasoning or understanding. Remember, half of the truth mentally can be more damaging than the truth itself.

Once again, it is because the mind will struggle to fill in the missing pieces. It doesn't matter how intense or how strenuous the efforts, without going to the source, your work may be futile. You see, to remove the guesswork, we need the source to provide the necessary information; therefore, solving the problems becomes easy. There are times when living with your spouse is so confusing, the marriage is full of misunderstanding and because of the anger and hostility the two of you feel more like combatants than husband and wife. He or she happens to be one big mystery. You no longer understand the complexity of each other's thinking. You can't figure out why they're not completely understanding what you are trying to get across.

> There is only one truth, but few perceive what the truth really is.

We need to learn that passing judgment, criticizing, and making threats based on a portion of the facts is not intelligent or wise. Every man's way is right in his own eyesight. We could save ourselves a lot of grief if we learn to look at things from the other side or the other point of view. The truth could be simple, complex, or difficult. One must learn to look at all sides of the truth before drawing a conclusion to a problem. If we practice this, we can extinguish a lot of the small fires erupting within our marriages. We must retrain ourselves to look at things from all sides not just the side holding our pain. Problems continue in marriage because we are steadfast looking at things from our side only. Please understand, I am not talking about clearly defined dos and don'ts, rights or wrongs, I am talking about perception.

Classic example: You discovered a mark on the collar of his shirt. It looks like lipstick. You logically assume he is having an affair. "How could he!" you say. You cut up his shirts, strip his bank accounts, break the plasma television, throw his music CD's away, and sell his golf clubs all before he arrives home from work.

*Read along with me:*

Author: You need facts of an affair. Lipstick is not evidence of an affair nor is it enough to convict him or to find him guilty of anything.

Wife: Well, I know a woman is involved! Why was she hugging him? What is a woman's lipstick doing on his collar? I can't even get him to hug me!

Author: Okay, let's conclude that it is a woman's lipstick. Who is the woman?

Wife: It doesn't matter! I don't care! She had no business with her hands on my husband!

Author: It does matter! What if the lipstick belongs to his mother, sister, or daughter? Would it matter then? Of course, it would matter. With that said, let's say the lipstick belongs to his sister.

Wife: Yet still, why was it there?

Author: An innocent, good-bye embrace

Wife: Oops!

Author: You are right. Oops!

Every situation is not as innocent as the one I described. You are the one with the knowledge about your spouse. This simple exercise is only to point out how easy it is to make a mistake and draw the wrong conclusion looking at things from one side only.

There could be several reasons for the lipstick on his collar:

1. He is truly having an affair.

2. The co-worker was suicidal. The embrace was for emotional support.

3. A family friend received tragic, devastating news. The embrace was a sign of sympathy and compassion.

4. The lipstick was on a friend's hand and without knowledge, his hand or her hand attempted to straighten out his collar leaving the mark.

5. While in a restaurant, an overly friendly, old waitress placed her hand on his shoulder area unaware she was leaving the mark.

6. The mark could be from a dipstick and not lipstick.

My point is this. The wife can accept the source's explanation for the mark or she can look inward for the answer. But what if he is lying? The better question would be. What if he's telling the truth? By thinking he's lying, the mind will continue searching for the missing or the unknown. But if he is telling the truth and conditions worsen within the relationship, it is your thinking that's creating the prolonged problems not the innocent mark on his collar.

- Why do you think the way you do?

- Why do you think the worst?

- Why do you see the negatives?

- Why won't you change your views?

- Why is their thinking wrong?

- Why is your thinking right?

I am not suggesting that anyone be naïve. So, what if your fears and suspicions are correct? What if he has been dishonest as well as having an affair? The proper response is to face the facts and deal with the facts accordingly. This simple exercise was to point out that some individuals have a natural tendency of receiving information based on their interpretation of a subject matter.

## Room To Grow

If you have been married for several years, it is safe for me to say the person you married, however many years ago, is not the same person you're married to today. All of us are going through our own metamorphosis. Your spouse is no exception; they are evolving. Their views, beliefs and needs are consistently changing, and it is vital you adjust to him or her.

It is important you know yourself. If you are a person that resists change, it's important you recognize that fact because your resistance to change may continue to create problems for the two of you. You cannot allow your lack of growth to stifle the growth of your spouse. We spend an enormous amount of time dissecting the mannerisms of our spouse. What if that same amount of time, was spent focusing on our Self.

It has been said that there is some good in the worst of us and there is some bad in the best of us. It is the bad in you that he or she will reject, and it is the good in you he or she will embrace. You must know the good to present the good. When a woman pleases a man and a man pleases a woman it requires both parties, not just meeting needs, but attempting to understand why we, ourselves, need what we think we need.

## Confronting You

- Do you know what will produce happiness for you?

- Whose opinion of you matters?

- Do you truly want what you say you want?

- In life, what truly matters?

- Do you know you?

- Do you like you?

Each of us should develop a personal self-improvement course. We should strive to be the very best we possibly can be. As you can see, knowing *you* is a greater challenge than knowing your spouse. Maximize your knowledge of who you are. The things you desire out of life could already be present in your life simply awaiting your recognition of them.

## Key Points

- Knowing oneself is as equally important as knowing your spouse.

- Self-understanding is the way to personal contentment within your relationship.

- To have your needs met, you must first identify what your needs are.

- You can't be all that you can be until you first confront you, know you, understand you, and if necessary change you.

- One must learn to look at all sides of the truth before drawing a conclusion to a problem.

- We begin to help ourselves when we begin to understand ourselves.

- Looking inward is just as important as looking outward.

# The Journey Continues...

Thirteen

# THE FORBIDDEN FRUIT

> For Adam and Eve, the forbidden was the fruit of a tree. For every *committed relationship*, the forbidden is another man or woman. Like Eve, the forbidden is inviting, but the bite of the forbidden is self-destructive. The forbidden will take you further than you wanted to go and cost you more than you wanted to pay.

This chapter is written with the following groups of individuals in mind.

- Those who truly love our Lord and Savior Jesus Christ,

- Those who have passed or failed a test of temptation.

- Those in a monogamous relationship, man or woman, who hold the marital vows dear and sacred.

- Those who are one hundred percent in love and committed to the person they married.

- Those naïve to the subtleness of being lured away by temptation.

- Those that have never faced or dwelt with serious temptation.

- Those that think you or your spouse are above temptation.

- Those entering or exiting serious temptation.

- Singles enjoying the forbidden fruit.

This chapter is to enlighten you, but most of all warn you about the dangers of the forbidden fruit. Today, just like in the Garden of Eden, the power to resist the fruit remains a challenge.

Nevertheless, man has been warned since the beginning of time about the forbidden fruit.

Genesis 3:2-3

*"And the woman said unto the serpent, we may eat of the fruit of the trees of the garden but of the fruit of the tree which is in the mist of the garden, God hath said, ye shall not eat of it neither shall ye touch it, lest ye die."*

## The Forbidden Fruit

The fruit is only a symbol of one's desires. It is anything wanted, yearned, or ached for. The word forbidden places a restriction on the observer rendering the object of one's affection - off limits! No one can claim to be exempt from temptation. The permissible and the forbidden fruit can be side by side. However, if controlled by the flesh, into the forbidden is where we will sink our teeth. Our nature craves or desires that which is off limits, or we desire things that are bad for us. All of us must guard ourselves against the indulgences of our flesh.

Remove desire and there can be no temptation. As a result, there is no struggle to uphold a religious belief or a promise made. Replace the desire, and the temptation is once again possible. Simply put, if you have no sexual interest in a woman or a man there is no temptation to violate your marital vows. What happens when everything you want in the opposite sex is staring you in the face or it's something about them you just can't shake,

Maybe it's their fragrance, the way they look at you, their voice, their laughter, emotional state, their predicament, or maybe it's a body feature or some unique quality about them. And to further complicate things, they have made themselves available to you. A mistake in handling this situation could cause your temptation meter to rise. Is the problem with the other person or is it you? What are you missing within that's seeking an outside connection? Is it possible that what you admire about them is already at home, but has been overlooked?

In the Garden of Eden, biting the fruit produced spiritual death for man. Likewise, if you are married, biting the forbidden fruit will produce death for your union or bring death into your union. Death of intimacy, trust, respect, and communication. There is a reason why the fruit is forbidden in the first place. Now, let's return to the Garden of Eden.

## Was The Fruit Bad Or Evil?

There was nothing wrong with the fruit. It wasn't evil or corrupt. God declared everything He created was good. Adam and Eve would suffer no immediate physical consequences as a result of eating the fruit. They were in trouble because of disobedience. The serpent presented, and Eve consented. The problem was with Adam and Eve yielding to what was offered to them. News flash! Everything offered to you is not necessarily good for you. From a humanistic standpoint, being blessed with attractive features or having the opposite sex admire some quality about you does not make one evil or bad. It is what you do with the knowledge of knowing they are attracted to you.

## King David And The Forbidden Fruit

2 Samuel 11:2-5

*"And it came to pass in an evening tide that David arose from off his bed; and walked upon the roof of the king's house and from the roof he saw a woman washing herself; and the woman was very beautiful to look upon. And David sent and inquired after the woman. And one said, is not this Bath-she-ba, the daughter of E-li-am, the wife of U-ria-ah the Hitite? And David sent messengers,*

*and took her; and she came in unto him, and he lay with her; for she was purified from her uncleanness: And she returned unto her house. And the woman conceived, and sent and told David, and said, I am with Child."*

In some minds, Bath-she-ba may appear to be a poor, innocent victim who was taken advantage of by a powerful king, but if you read this story carefully Bath-she-ba could have set the king up concerning their night of physical intimacy.

## Some Of My Questions Concerning Bath-she-ba:

1. Why was she bathing in open view of the king?

2. Did she not know that the open view would be a source of temptation for King David?

3. Could her bathing be a part of some plan on her part?

4. Why didn't she resist David's advances?

5. Since David saw her bathing, was she watching David as she bathed? If so, did she enjoy him looking at her bathe?

## The Steps To David's Downfall

| | | |
|---|---|---|
| 1. | Arose from his bed | no sin there |
| 2. | Walked upon his roof top | no sin there |
| 3. | Saw a woman washing herself | start of his problem |
| 4. | Lusted for her | flesh acting up |
| 5. | Sent to inquire of her | discovered she was married |
| 6. | Sent and took her | yielding to the desire |
| 7. | Sexual encounter with her | sin |

David:   the hand-picked king

David:   the apple of God's eye

David:   one of God's best

David knew Bath-she-ba was a married woman and that she belonged to another man, yet he desired her, took her, and had a sexual encounter with her. David's body desired Bath-she-ba. He wanted to satisfy his flesh by indulging his flesh. Like an aching tooth or a man in a hot desert, his body and emotions throbbed for relief. His flesh was yelling, screaming, crying, and begging David to satisfy the yearning. Repeatedly, David hears, *I want her!* Maybe his spirit says no, but his flesh says, YES, YES, GIVE HER TO ME. Like an itching back desiring to be scratched or a spoiled child throwing a temper tantrum, David's flesh is demanding to yield to the temptation. GIVE HER TO ME NOW! I WANT HER!

Again, the bite of pleasure is simply the after effects of being satisfied or charmed by a woman or a man. The after affects can be good or bad. During this period, the chemistry and bond between the two appear unbreakable. If the two were separated by time, distance, or death the connection still would not be dissolved. The individuals in question would experience a lifetime of yearning.

For this story and far too many other stories, the flesh prevailed. It's true, King David had other love interests, but the excitement, mental thoughts, and lustful craving all added to the emotional battles King David faced. His insane state was, in part, because Bath-she-ba was forbidden. After their night of forbidden passion, Bath-she-ba conceives a child and David attempts to hide the pregnancy. In his failed attempts, he has her husband killed. (2 Samuel 11:14-17)

When a man truly fears God, before he disappoints God with such unrighteous acts of adultery and murder, there will be a struggle within the soul of that man. Righteous men and women do not just walk into sinful situations or deliberately sin. There will always be a fight, a struggle, or a battle. Fighting sexual temptation is not a two or three-minute ordeal, then it's over for the day. Contrary to what one may believe, this struggle is 24/7.

Your body is screaming at you to satisfy its desires. One can escape a burning building or a deadly situation, but how can one escape their flesh? The spirit is saying," No!" Your mouth is saying, "No, because I am married. No, because I love my spouse. No, because I love God. No, because it's wrong. No, because of my title. Nonetheless, your overcharged emotions are saying YES! Like King David, your body is yelling or screaming at you to yield to the temptation.

Flesh cares nothing about your marital status or how long you have been married. It cares nothing about your title or position in the community or society. Years ago, a popular commercial said the only way to get rid of a temptation is to yield to it. I do not share that belief. For men and women of integrity, yielding is not an option. The desire to do the right thing is what's producing the struggle. If there were no desire to do right, there would be no mental battle. Have you noticed the first four letters of Bath-she-ba's name spells, bath? It's ironic her sin with David involves a bath. What David *saw* started everything.

There is one lesson we can certainly take away from David and Bath-she-ba and that is every woman, especially married women, needs to be very careful how she's viewed through the eyes of men. Married women should ask themselves if they are revealing too much leg, thigh, or breast for another man's eyes. If you are questioning whether an outfit is too tight or cut too low, perhaps it is. If you were to ask some males, their answer would be an unequivocally yes!

For the man that's struggling with the lure of the opposite sex, they do not need the added temptation. Your body is off limits to him so help him by presenting yourself in a suitable manner. If a man can determine whether you are wearing thongs or regular underwear, it's too tight. If your dress is low cut and your breast keep falling out of your bra, you are sending the wrong message. God designed you in a way that's already desirable and appealing to men, so when a man sees partial nudity or total nudity, it has the potential to bewilder his mind. Married women should be reserved and certainly dress more conservatively. If you are married you are the forbidden fruit, and every other male or female is forbidden fruit for you.

Most of our attention in this chapter has been focused on the forbidden fruit. I would like to now spend some time discussing the permitted fruit. The husband and wife should fulfill the righteous sexual desires of each other. If you withhold sex from your partner, you are opening the door for sexual temptation. All other forms of temptation will come from a forbidden source. You are the only place your spouse can go for moral sexual pleasure.

## Singles And The Forbidden Fruit

Sometime ago, I was talking with a young man in his early twenties who was reflecting on his wrongful sexual encounters. He mentioned he constantly found himself in bed with married women. The fact these women were married was of no concern to him. The only thing that mattered was they wanted him, and he wanted sex. The married women were to blame, but the young man was guilty as well. This young man was warned about his wrongful deeds; however, he didn't take heed to the warnings. At the time of my conversation with this young man, he was dealing with the sting of spousal adultery. He learned a very important lesson about sowing and reaping. Reaping sometimes cuts to the bone.

Single men and women need to respect the marital union despite the actions of the participants within that union. Yes, they are the ones in a committed relationship; however, you are still responsible for *your* actions. If you are single, a married woman or man is the forbidden fruit. There is a price to be paid for sinking one's teeth into the forbidden fruit. Is it worth it? Is it worth your relationship, your standing in the community, your name, throwing away fifteen or twenty years of marriage? Is it worth losing your home, children, or your future? All the devil's fruit has worms.

## Consider The Worms Of The Forbidden Fruit

- David and Bath-she-ba's child died
- Unwanted pregnancies
- Divorce
- AIDS
- STDs
- Prolonged martial trouble
- Loss of intimacy, honor and respect
- Financial problems
- Child support
- Private and public embarrassment

From a flesh standpoint, to some extent I can understand committing adultery if the following occurred when you had sexual relations with different women.

- You're having sexual relations and real flames shot out of her backside or his backside.

- Another woman or man caused the Earth to literally shake underneath the two of you.

- Another woman or man caused you to literally see stars.

- With another the orgasms last for an hour.

But, you know what? Generally, the feeling is the same. Still, lovemaking is better with your husband or wife. It's better because it's morally and spiritually right. So, the question is, how do you win this struggle? First, let's establish the fact that temptation is not a sin - yielding to temptation is. Satan's pattern is for you to see, desire, and take.

I John 2:16 (paraphrase)

*The lust of the eyes seeing*
*The lust of the flesh desiring*
*Pride of life taking to have for oneself*

Eve saw the fruit, desired it, and took it. David saw Bath-she-ba's nakedness, desired to have her, and took her.

1 Corinthians 10:13

*"There hath no temptation taken you but such as common to man: but God is faithful, who will not suffer you to be tempted above that ye are able, but will with the temptation also make a way to escape, that ye may be able to bear it."*

God will provide an exit for you, a way of escape. He will not put any more on you than you are able to bear. The load may appear to be too heavy and the ordeal too hard to endure but remember God knows your load limit and he will limit your load.

Jesus Christ was also tempted by Satan, (Matthew 4:1-11) yet he did not sin, he resisted, and the devil departed. Several significant features stand out as one contemplates Jesus' temptation in the wilderness. His encounter with the devil in the wilderness is a source of encouragement and instruction to believers as they battle temptation.

Several significant features stand out as one contemplates Jesus' temptation in the wilderness. His encounter with the devil in the wilderness is a source of encouragement and instruction to believers as they battle temptation.

- His commitment to the fathers will

- Use of scripture

- His resolve to resist the devil

James 4:7

*"Submit yourself then to God. Resist the devil and he will flee you."*

Resist thinking about him or her. Resist proper or improper thoughts about him or her. Resist communicating with him or her. Starve your flesh so the tempter and the temptation can flee. You can't escape your flesh, but you can crucify it. To every man/woman who has found themselves in this chapter, yes, you made mistakes, and even did some things wrong, but if you passed the test by not yielding to the sinful desires of your flesh I salute you. I applaud you!

Back to the Garden of Eden. The serpent, in his attempt to deceive Eve, would have been unsuccessful if God's manifested presence was in the garden. There is no way, Eve would have eaten the forbidden if God's manifested presence was in the garden, nor would she had presented it to Adam. Children wait until they're away from their parents to misbehave; Adam and Eve were no exceptions. This teaches us that having God's presence in our life is monumental in avoiding or overcoming temptation. Although His presence makes the difference, the final choice will always be ours. In the garden, Adam and Eve were questioned and punished by God. The consequences are the reward of poor choices.

## Key Points

- You are not above or exempt from temptation.

- There can be no temptation without desire.

- He who can't control himself gives control to another.

- Struggling means you are still fighting. Fighting represents resistance.

- The fruit was forbidden for a reason, to avoid the devil's worms leave the bait alone.

- You can pass the test of temptation.

- Conquer your desires or your desires will conquer you.

- Temptation is not a sin, yielding to temptation is.

- He who wins the fight within is worthy to lead other men.

# Conclusion

# HAPPILY EVER AFTER

Pleasure: enjoyment, delight and joy.

"All men have a taste for pleasure."

In the Garden of Eden, Adam was not tricked or deceived, yet he ate of the forbidden fruit. Why would Adam give up eternal life/paradise? Eve pleased Adam (power of persuasion); therefore, he wanted to please her. He surrendered to the emotional influence Eve held over him.

- The bite of pleasure for sports fans is more sports

- The bite of pleasure for movie goers is more movies

- The bite of pleasure for music lovers is more music

- The bite of pleasure for a man or woman is more of that man or woman, it is an insatiable appetite to please him/her

Your relationship is in your hands, and in your hands, is the ability to refresh, rekindle and to resuscitate your love.

## Bitten

For those who are scripturally joined together.

If the overwhelming subject matter resonated with you and your desire is for a healthier marriage, the following written prayer is dedicated to you and yours. This prayer can be recited jointly or alone. Standing before a lit candle, (preferably husband & wife) recite the following prayer.

## MARITAL PRAYER

Heavenly Father, forgive me and my spouse for the committed offenses to your word and to this union. Let the healing hands of heaven heal our marital ills. Refresh the areas that are stale, rekindle the flames of love, and resuscitate that which is about to die. Let peace, love and honor strengthen our union each day as we adhere to the laws of marriage. From this day forward, we bury the past and walk in the newness of our love. Amen!

# A MESSAGE FROM THE AUTHOR

I am confident that our time together has not been in vain. My continual prayer is that God will renew all that needs to be renewed in your life. In sincerity, I believe the blessings of God are to be shared. We're blessed to be a blessing!

Marriage is under attack, and as you can see from the statistics below, the institution of marriage is in trouble, but we can reverse this trend.

- The marriage rate is declining in the U.S. Fewer people are married and those that do get married are marrying later in life (age 30 for men- age 25 for women).

- Only 63% of men claim to be happy in marriage, while 60.7 % of women make such a claim.

- 41 % of first marriages end in divorce.

- 60% of second marriages end in divorce.

- 73% of third marriages end in divorce.

- In America, divorce occurs every 36 seconds, 2,400 per day, 16,800 per week, and 876,000 per year.

(www.mckinleyirvin.com)

## Pushing Marriage Forward Crusade

I am asking you to join my crusade to save a marriage by sharing *The Bite of Pleasure* with singles and married or engaged couples you know. If you benefitted from *The Bite of Pleasure*, encourage someone else to purchase the book/workbook.

Something as simple as sharing my Facebook page or retweeting a tweet may help save someone's marriage; it's already happening! Your labor of love will not be forgotten. Will you join my crusade to save a marriage and uplift someone living single? If so, visit my webpage to let me know! (www.authoreddiefray.weebly.com)

# COOKIE COMMITMENT

Ladies, the Cookie Commitment begins with you. It begins with understanding your overwhelming value as a woman. It begins with making a commitment to yourself - a commitment to honor your body. The commitment begins with a set of non-compromising values, standards and morals. Standards are important because standards are a guide, an inner voice to direct you. Your standards are your shield of protection. Although you may have lost this important aspect, God and man realize you are the greatest of all creation.

It is not my place or any other man's place to set a date/time limit for your first sexual encounter with a man; however, some of you have been blessed with a parent who has a God-given right to help you learn to conduct yourself at a high standard. Always remember, God has the *highest* standards for you.

Please, hear me. In a non-working environment, 98% of the men (in theory) who approach you are cookie driven. Their number one goal is to get the cookie. Wake up! The goal of the referenced man is not to establish a long-term relationship with you, advance your life, financially support you, or to love or understand you. No! His goal is to get the cookie. To get the cookie, we become who we need to become (role player) and we say what needs to be said. Allow me to share another secret with you...men see it as A GAME OF CHESS, A GAME OF LIES AND MANIPULATION, and A GAME OF DECEIT AND DECEPTION.

Real men value the cookie! *However, the value we set should not be greater than the value you place on the cookie.* Ladies, if loyalty and dedication is your aim, consider the Cookie Commitment. The Cookie Commitment fosters commitment.

# ABOUT THE AUTHOR

Eddie Lee Fray has been married to the same women for 37 years and is the proud father of three beautiful young ladies. He lived most of his adult life in a small community outside of Houston, Texas and now resides in his native state of Florida in the city of Pensacola. He is the senior pastor of Life Changing Ministries (Pensacola) and is called to share God's Word and God's standard for marriage – uncompromisingly. Pastor Fray is also a successful entrepreneur, songwriter, recording artist, poet, and an inventor with a product currently on the market.

Pastor Fray has chosen to donate a portion of the proceeds from this book to two organizations he's given to over the years which are the Steve and Marjorie Harvey Foundation and Truth for Youth Ministries (Rev. John Powell).

To schedule Pastor Fray to share his message with your group or organization, please visit www.authoreddiefray.com or email edcyntfray1@bellsouth.net for more information.

www.ingramcontent.com/pod-product-compliance
Lightning Source LLC
Chambersburg PA
CBHW021102090426
42738CB00006B/464